Terra Australis

TERRA AUSTRALIS

✦ LF BOLLÉE & PHILIPPE NICLOUX ✦
TRANSLATED BY EDWARD GAUVIN

"Throughout the world my homeland lies
I'll never witness with these eyes
its end, for this our world is round."

Tristan Corbière, "Pariah", from *Yellow Loves*.

SELF
MADE
HERO

First published in English 2014
by SelfMadeHero
5 Upper Wimpole Street
London W1G 6BP
www.selfmadehero.com

Written by: LF Bollée
Illustrated by: Philippe Nicloux
Translated by: Edward Gauvin

Editorial & Production Manager: Lizzie Kaye
Sales & Marketing Manager: Sam Humphrey
Publishing Director: Emma Hayley
With thanks to: Nick de Somogyi and Jane Laporte

ROYAUME-UNI

This book is supported by the Institut français (Royaume-Uni)
as part of the Burgess programme.

A CIP record for this book is available from the British Library

ISBN: 978-1-906838-75-1

10 9 8 7 6 5 4 3 2 1

Printed and bound in China

INTRODUCTION
by LF Bollée

"When dawn and dream agree to name a victor..." Odd, how these beautiful words, borrowed from a Henning Mankell thriller I read recently, come to mind at the very moment I am begging your indulgence for a few brief remarks about what an adventure *Terra Australis* has been. There's no real connection between modern-day Sweden and newborn Australia at the end of the 18th century, but I liked the line, and I liked writing the book you now hold in your hands even more.

One day, I got up at dawn sure of one thing: the prospect of a long voyage lay before me, and I'd better not miss the boat. A pressing, imperious summons! The form it would take was still vague, but there was no doubt as to the destination: that far-off land whose outline everyone knows, an island but also a continent (or vice versa), which had always been a kind of lodestone, drawing my thoughts and dreams…

The Australia I first dreamed of as a teenager, convinced I'd need to go there someday.

The Australia I later explored as an adult, certain it would haunt me forever.

The Australia I finally set down on paper, so as not to let it slip away. I believe I love it immoderately.

To begin with, the legend goes something like this: a nation born from a shipful of convicts. A gaggle of criminals sentenced to transportation who washed up onshore, knowing neither how nor why, who settled largely hostile territories and wound up staying, all while disregarding the indigenous peoples there already. A bit vague as stories go, isn't it? And all the more paradoxical given how recent it is: we must try and imagine that on the very first Bastille Day, there were barely a thousand people and a handful of improvised dwellings above the beach that, today, is Sydney Ferry Terminal. What were those people doing there? Why had they been sent to Botany Bay (a name commonly used, despite being mistaken right from the start)? How did cohabitation with the "natives" (not yet known as aborigines) really go down; who was in charge and how did they get organized? So many questions we largely ignore, so many answers to supply. Especially since, where the French are concerned, a certain Monsieur Lapérouse was apparently present right from the start... yes, really! You'll see: even if that far corner of the earth was called Terra Australis Incognita, from 1770 to 1791 it was an irresistible magnetic pole, a veritable social, political, and geographical black hole, drawing and focusing all humanity's energies. The face of the world changed, and the Pacific was its mirror, in which it suddenly no longer recognized itself.

Let me say up front: I don't know who the good guys were, the bad guys, the torturers, the victims, the saints, the demons. All I know is that men march forward and seldom take the time to look around them. I know they are weak and unjust, capable of the noblest impulses and the darkest thoughts. I know that wherever they go, they carry within them the deadliest diseases and the deepest doubts. I suppose it is in their essence to do wrong, and in their nature to regret it. I think we can try and plumb the depths of their souls.

This book was born in December 2007.

A cliff walk on Phillip Island, south of Melbourne. Flies by the dozen, buzzing in air fanned by warm winds, and in my nonstop attempts to fend them off, a thought crept in: Phillip Island... wait a minute, just who is Phillip?

Arthur Phillip (1738-1814), naval officer, commander of the First Fleet, first English governor of New South Wales. One year of reading and research to find out more, to begin to understand the individuals, groups, subgroups, ramifications, relations, chronologies, events... An initial 800-page draft that had to be cut, painfully... Lunch with my editor Franck Marguin, who did me the friendly favour not only of hearing me out, but of seeming fascinated by this moment of history. And who has accompanied me on this journey ever since, offering unfailing support and unerring advice. Thank you, dear friend; you have my eternal gratitude for the trust you placed in me and for being the first to believe in this book. I hope I was worthy of your trust and friendship.

Warm, affectionate thoughts for all the staff at Glénat, who accompanied me on the open and often stormy seas: Jacques, Jean, Philippe, Christian, Cécile, Élise, Fanny, Mathilde, Étienne – forgive me if I've forgotten anyone.

Thanks to the Australians who were free with information and, in various ways, helped me out: Annie Campbell of the Museum of Sydney, Richard Ogier of the Australian Embassy in France, Eddie Campbell, George Vlastras, Stephen

Ford of Kings Comics in Sydney, Kirsten Orr, Roger Faulkner, Shauna Kane, Aaron Noonan, Roland Dane. Special thanks to Admiral François Bellec, and to the efficient mediation of Brieg F. Haslé.

Who else? Who had the courage and the nerve to follow me for five years, a performance all the more remarkable since he has not, to this day, set foot on Australian soil? "To write is to listen," famous French comics creator Christian Godard told me one day. I owe my start in the world of writing comics to him, and my thoughts turn to him today. Yes, I listened to my characters talk, I transcribed their words, tried to capture the attitudes I could make out through the documents at my disposal. But in this case, listening was not enough. I also had to imagine, shape, sculpt, lend things and beings an appearance. I needed, in this instance, to meet my characters, almost live beside them, feel them moving around in my office, watch them pitch and sway with the stormy winds of their lives… Here I can reveal that artists Cyril Pedrosa, Matthieu Bonhomme, Shaun Tan, Andreas, and Marc Védrines were approached for this graphic novel. But schedules and the passing years impose constraints that vanquish even the best intentions.

One day, I was told a certain Philippe Nicloux had written a letter proposing himself as the artist for this book. I never knew how he found out, and how he got the crazy idea into his head, but I wasn't going to complain. A full-scale field test of four pages was given to this young father from Nice who already had two splendid books from the publisher Les Enfants Rouges to his credit. Four pages isn't much, right? Still, I admit it was too early for me, I hadn't finished tinkering with the book's structure. I wrote a short sequence sure to make it into the final draft: the departure of the

fleet from Portsmouth at dawn on 13 May 1787, featuring a wigless Arthur Phillip with butterflies in his stomach at the challenge awaiting him. I have always maintained that he must have been dying of fear and anxiety as he was leaving; he must have smacked his forehead on the table where he was sitting and said something like, "God give me strength!" But the mise-en-scène still had a long way to go. To cut a long story short, Philippe Nicloux drew the sequence, and I was… disappointed. Disappointed because I saw my layouts weren't appropriate for a graphic novel whose rhythm would naturally be unusual. Disappointed because Philippe presented me with my own failure, and it was also a way of saying that his art needed more, deserved better. The vagaries of any artistic effort, I suppose, when the foundations are still shaky…

But something else had happened, which almost contradicted the first: I had instantly understood that only Philippe Nicloux could draw *Terra Australis*, and that we would soon be setting sail together… That flamboyant black line; those faces, sometimes deformed but ever so expressive; those figures, forceful and fragile at once; and those great shivering trees, those menacing hulks, those buffeted boats and mysterious forests that I had unconsciously been waiting for right from the story. Philippe would bring these all to me, things both vanished and still living, backdrops intimate and grandiose, characters big and small, atmospheres dark and bloody. There wasn't a single batch of pages from Philippe that Franck Marguin and I didn't wax ecstatic over – the sheer quality of the work – and I can still remember the frisson I felt each time I found I'd received mail from Philippe. I can never do justice to what I owe you, my friend and comrade, but I am forever grateful, and I hope we never stop. As Crowded

House, one of my favourite Australasian bands, once sang, there was "Something so strong..."

"When dawn and dream agree to name a victor..." Dawn can give birth to a sad and rainy day, dreams can turn into nightmares, nothing is ever fully won. But we need ambitions, beginnings. These two things brought this book into being, a book I hope you'll like. Don't hesitate to join us at the Terra Australis Facebook page, which we specially created as an extension of this voyage through history and time. Up till now, this voyage has been mainly in French, but something tells me this book's international adventure is just beginning...

One last word: while this book was being created, more than 200 people died in Australia due to terrible wildfires that devastated the Melbourne region in 2009 and the floods that struck the state of Queensland in 2010 and 2011. Two tragedies that remind us how much this land beyond dreamtime is a land of dangers and challenges. We will not forget these victims. To them, too, we dedicate this book: *Terra Australis.*

LF Bollée - 30 August 2012

Prologue

WILD.

FIERCE.

BURNING.

HOSTILE.

DISTANT.

ANCIENT.

NAKED. OCHRE.

GREEN.

SEA BLUE.

VIRGIN. VIOLENT.

MY LAND IS REMOTE,
SHELTERED FROM PRYING GAZE,
FROM TAINT AND HATRED.

I WANDER IT DAZED, DRUNK ON ITS BEAUTY,
MAD WITH ITS SOLITUDE.

I TAME THE SECRET OF THESE PROUD LATITUDES.

THE SUN WILL SOON DISAPPEAR. THE MILD EVENING BRINGS A BRIEF RESPITE...

I ROVE AND OBSERVE.

I LOOK AND LISTEN...

MY KIND HAVE LIVED HERE SINCE THE DAWN OF TIME.

FIRST AND FINAL TRUTH.

I DON'T EVEN KNOW IF MY LAND HAS BORDERS.

I DISAPPEAR INTO THE WOODS AND SENSE ANOTHER PRESENCE.

THEY'RE HERE.

THEM.

THE DARK MEN.

THEY HAVE GATHERED. A RITUAL HAS BEGUN.

CHILDREN ON ONE SIDE, ADULTS ON THE OTHER.

I KNOW WHAT WILL HAPPEN.

MYSTERY OF FEARS.

FEAR OF MYSTERIES.

THE CEREMONY GOES ON AS DARKNESS GROWS.

THE BOYS CONTEMPLATE THE ACTIONS OF THEIR FATHERS.

THEIR ANCESTORS DID THE SAME, IN THEIR DAY.

THE CHILDREN WILL BECOME ADULTS...

BUT IT IS THE ELDERS WHO SEEM TO BE PLAYING LIKE CHILDREN.

THEY SHOW THEIR CHILDREN THE WAY.

THEY TELL THEM THEY WILL LOSE THEIR INNOCENCE.

I AM NOT SURE
I WANT TO STAY.

AMONG THE DARK MEN,
LOSS OF INNOCENCE IS
PAID FOR DEARLY.

THE BOYS WILL SUFFER,
AND THEIR CRIES BECOME
LOST IN THE NIGHT.

I RESUME MY WANDERING. I FIND THE WOODS MORE WELCOMING.

THE TREES ARE MY BRETHREN.

SOON I CAN FEEL A LIGHT BREEZE FROM THE BEACH.

I HEAR THE PEACEFUL STIRRING OF THE OCEAN.

ITS PERPETUAL POSITIONING.

FOR SOME TIME NOW IT HAS TOLERATED A DISTANT VISITOR.

THE GREAT SHIP OF
THE WHITE MEN.

18

AND I WONDER WHAT COULD BE AFOOT...

THEY CALL ME HANGING JOHNNIE!

INSIDE THIS WORLD...

HOORAY! HOORAY!

THAT I DO NOT YET KNOW...

THEY SAY I HANG FOR MONEY!

23

WE'LL DO THE OL' FELLA UP RIGHT NICE.

HOLD HIM GOOD. THIS'LL HURT.

MAGRA, YOU BASTARD, WHAT EXACTLY D'YE HAVE IN MIND?

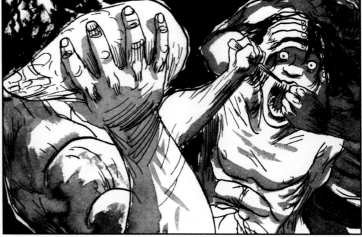

24

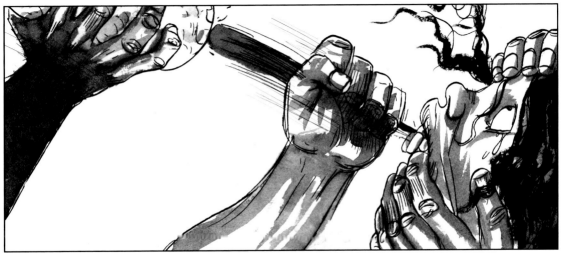

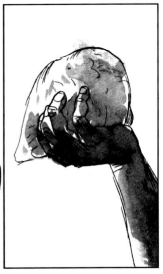

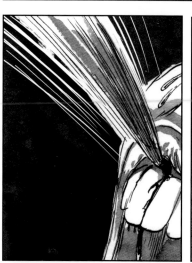

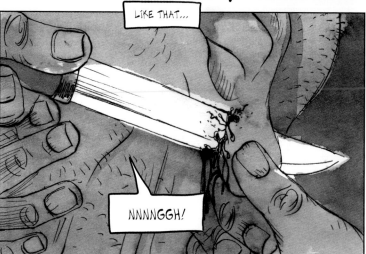

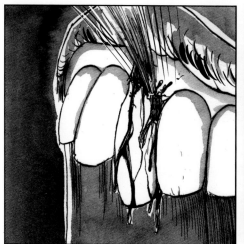

26

ABSOLUTELY UNACCEPTABLE, MR. MAGRA!

I KNOW YOU'LL DENY THE CHARGE OF THE CRIME COMMITTED AGAINST MR. ORTON LAST NIGHT.

I KNOW HE WON'T RISK IDENTIFYING YOU FORMALLY.

I ALSO KNOW YOU WEREN'T ALONE LAST NIGHT.

BUT I HAVE GOOD REASON TO SUSPECT YOU, MR. MAGRA!

IT'S NOT THE FIRST TIME SOMEONE'S REPORTED YOUR ACTIVITIES...

WHEN YOU'RE THE WORSE FOR DRINK AND LIKE PLAYING WITH KNIVES.

I CANNOT TOLERATE SUCH INCIDENTS, SUCH MUTILATIONS, ABOARD THE *ENDEAVOUR*.

THEY REPRESENT THE GREATEST INSULT TO MY AUTHORITY OVER THIS VESSEL.

AS A RESULT, I AM PROVISIONALLY RELIEVING YOU FROM YOUR DUTIES AS MIDSHIPMAN. THE POOP IS FORBIDDEN TO YOU.

YOU MAY GO.

AYE, CAPTAIN.

"THAT MAGRA IS, TO PUT IT BLUNTLY, WORTHLESS..."

I LEAVE THE MEN ON THE SHIP TO THEIR STORIES, THEIR MISERIES, AND THEIR STRANGE CUSTOMS...

SOON THEY WILL TAKE THEIR LEAVE... NEVER TO RETURN, I HOPE.

I RETURN TO THE WOODS...

AND I SEE THAT THE DARK MEN HAVE CONTINUED THEIR RITES OF INITIATION THROUGH THE NIGHT.

THERE ARE TWO CHILDREN LEFT, LYING ON THE GROUND.

ONE SEEMS IN TERRIBLE PAIN. THE OTHER IS UNCONSCIOUS, PERHAPS EVEN DEAD.

MY LIFE IS HERE.

MY ROOTS PLUNGE INTO THIS LAND
THAT NATURE HAS GIVEN TO MY KIND.

MY FRIENDS, MY BROTHERS, WE ARE
THE TRUE PEOPLE OF THIS LAND!

WE ARE AT HOME HERE.
OUR BODIES ARE ONE WITH
THESE PLACES AND LANDSCAPES
THAT ARE THE EXTENSION AND
REFLECTION OF OUR EXISTENCE.

Book I
Distant Horizons

"In our cities vast, does fate men divide,
By two unjust laws, side from side."

André Chénier
(*Posthumous Poems*, circa 1782)

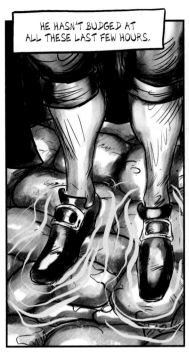

HE HASN'T BUDGED AT ALL THESE LAST FEW HOURS.

STIFF, AWKWARD, HEAVY, A STEM WITHOUT A FLOWER...

A GHOSTLY MAN WHOSE GAZE, HOLLOW AND SPENT, BESPEAKS A MIND RACKED BY BRUTAL TORMENT.

THESE CONVENT WALLS A WOMAN HOLD: HIS GOAL.

HIS HEART'S FEVER, THE POISON OF HIS SOUL.

WHAT A JULY, EH?
BEEN LIKE THIS FOR A WEEK!

HAVE A SEAT, MONSIEUR.
HOW ABOUT A NICE GLASS
OF RED?

THANK YOU.

IT'LL WARM YOUR SOUL,
EVEN IF IT DOESN'T DRY
YOUR CLOTHES!

43

AND I FROM LONDON. I WORK FOR THE.... HOME OFFICE.

HOW DO YOU SAY THAT IN FRENCH?

NO, NO, JUST JOKING. I HAIL FROM LANGUEDOC. MY FATHER LIVES THERE STILL.

THE "HOME OFFICE"? SOMETHING LIKE THE MINISTRY OF THE INTERIOR, NON?

OUI... I'M HERE ON A MISSION.

"YOU'RE NOT ABOUT TO TELL ME YOU'RE A SPY, ARE YOU?"

GOOD HEAVENS, NO! I AM A... HOW DO YOU SAY IT? A CIVIL SERVANT DISPATCHED ON AN ODD AFFAIR. I GO HOME TOMORROW.

AH, ENGLAND. I CONSIDER JAMES COOK TO BE ONE OF THE GREATEST MEN OF THE CENTURY.

COOK? THE EXPLORER?

BUT ALSO NAVIGATOR AND CARTOGRAPHER!

HIS MAPS AND CALCULATIONS ARE UNEQUALLED!

YOU'RE A NAVAL OFFICER!

DOES IT SHOW?

ONLY SAILORS HAVE SUCH MUTUAL ESTEEM THAT IT TRANSCENDS WARS AND NATIONS.

"NO DOUBT BECAUSE THE SEAS AND UNCHARTED LANDS BELONG TO EVERYONE!"

"THERE ARE MANY PLACES LEFT TO EXPLORE...."

AND GOD WILLING, I'LL BE A WORTHY SUCCESSOR TO YOUR CAPTAIN COOK SOMEDAY.

HE DIED TOO EARLY. CERTAINLY HIS... BÂTON (RIGHT?) NEEDS PASSING ON.

PERHAPS IT IS FRANCE'S TURN TO MOUNT A GREAT EXPEDITION AROUND THE WORLD, TO DISCOVER THE LEGENDARY TERRA AUSTRALIS.

THOMAS TOWNSHEND IS THE SON OF THOMAS TOWNSHEND SENIOR AND ALBINIA SELWYN.

MR. TOWNSHEND, WHO DIED THREE YEARS AGO, WAS THE 2ND SON OF CHARLES TOWNSHEND, THE 2ND VISCOUNT TOWNSHEND...

WHY IS THAT?

AND ELIZABETH PELHAM-HOLLES. NOW, THE SECRETARY ASKED ME TO INQUIRE INTO HIS PATERNAL GRANDMOTHER'S SIDE.

I SHOULDN'T REALLY SAY, BUT IT'S CLEARLY BECAUSE THERE'S NO TITLE ON THE TOWNSHEND SIDE...

WHEREAS PELHAM-HOLLES IS ANOTHER MATTER.

LOOK: ELIZABETH PELHAM-HOLLES IS THE DAUGHTER OF THOMAS PELHAM, THE 1ST BARON PELHAM, AND GRACE HOLLES, DAUGHTER OF THE 3RD EARL OF CLARE.

THOMAS PELHAM IS THE SON OF SIR JOHN PELHAM, 3RD BARONET OF THE NAME, WHO MARRIED LUCY, DAUGHTER OF THE 2ND EARL OF LEICESTER.

I'M NOT SURE I FOLLOW...

RIGHT, SORRY. THIS CAN'T BE VERY INTERESTING.

JUST KNOW THAT ACCORDING TO THE HOME SECRETARY...

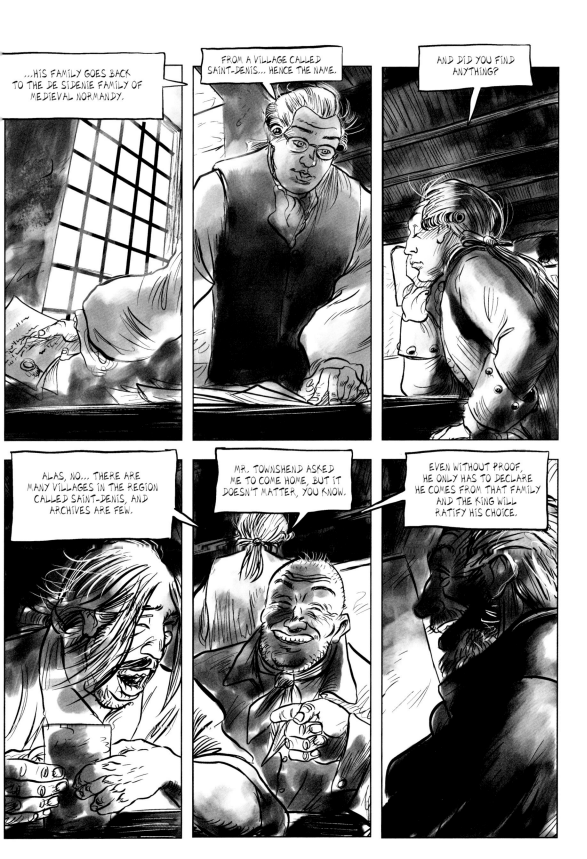

"IT'S STOPPED RAINING."

"I MUST BE ON MY WAY, THEY'RE WAITING FOR ME IN LONDON."

WHAT WILL YOU SAY TO YOUR FATHER?

I DON'T KNOW, BUT YOUR TALE HAS STIRRED CONFLICTING FEELINGS IN ME.

I'VE LEARNED THAT FAMILIES ARE ETERNAL, AND DIFFICULT TO FIGHT.

BUT ALSO THAT ALL FAMILY TREES ARE MARKED BY SHIFTS AND CHANGES...

BRANCHINGS AND NEW ROOTS THAT ARE QUITE SIMPLY...

THE INEVITABLE RESULT OF BREAKING AWAY.

IS THAT THE CONVENT?

YES, THE CONVENT OF SAINT-ÉTIENNE, A DOMINICAN ORDER.

MY SWEET ÉLÉONORE FOUND SANCTUARY THERE A FEW DAYS AGO. SHE ALWAYS SAID THAT IF SHE COULDN'T BE MY WIFE THEN SHE'D BE GOD'S.

BUT SHE WAS WRONG, AND I TOO.

MEETING YOU AND HEARING YOUR TALE HAS REMINDED ME THAT MEN ARE OFTEN MADE TO DEFY ESTABLISHED CONVENTIONS...

THAT THEIR TRUE NATURE LIES IN DISCOVERY AND ADVENTURE.

I AM SUCH A MAN!

WELL SAID!

OH, THIS RAIN! IT MIGHT CLEAN THINGS, BUT IT LEAVES YOUR FEET WET!

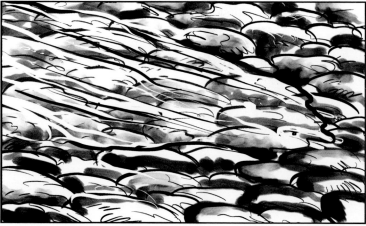

WHA—HEY!

HEY WHAT, PISSANT JOHNNY?

WEREN'T YOU THIRSTY?

WOKE YOU UP, RIGHT?

LOOKIT THE NITWIT!

YOU'RE ALL PIGS, THE LOT OF YOU! WORSE, EVEN!

HEH, WE SURE ARE. WORSE THAN YOU, JACKANAPES.

WHAT ELSE'D YOU CALL A KID WHO SLEEPS IN THE STREET AND NEVER BATHES?

WHO LIVES IN PISS AND SHIT AND GETS TOSSED AROUND ALL DAY LONG?

AN ANIMAL, JOHNNY! A GODFORSAKEN ANIMAL WHO'LL KEEL OVER ONE OF THESE DAYS WITHOUT EVER COMING TO GRIPS WI' HIS LIFE.

WELCOME TO LONDON!

HIS NAME WAS JOHN HUDSON.

HE WAS NINE.

HE WAS AN ORPHAN.

HE WAS SURVIVING.

NOT A BAD START.

JOHN HUDSON! SO THERE YOU ARE, YOU GUTTERSNIPE!

LOOK AT YOURSELF, YOU FLEA-RIDDEN CUR!

HEY! MY APPLE!

YOUR APPLE'S NOT WORTH A DAMN, IDIOT!

BUT IF YOU WORK FOR ME TODAY, YOU'LL EARN ENOUGH TO BUY ANOTHER!

I DON'T LIKE SWEEPING CHIMNEYS.

WHAT CHOICE DO YOU HAVE? YOU'VE NO OTHER WAY OF EARNING COIN!

YOU'RE LUCKY I HAVE YOUR BEST INTERESTS AT HEART! IT'S NOT EVERY DAY THERE'S WORK!

COME BACK AND SEE ME THIS AFTERNOON.

MEANWHILE, WASH YOUR FACE, WILL YOU? YOU LOOK LIKE A PICCANINNY. BAD FOR BUSINESS.

WHAT'S GOING ON?

PUBLIC EXECUTION!

YOU SURE?

SEE THE CART OVER THERE? HEADED FOR TYBURN!

GREAT! IT'S BEEN A WHILE!

LET'S GO AND SEE!

BETWEEN *1779* AND *1788*, THERE WERE 531 PUBLIC EXECUTIONS BY HANGING IN LONDON AND MIDDLESEX, MOST OFTEN AT THE "TYBURN TREE".

ON AVERAGE, ONE EVERY SIX DAYS.

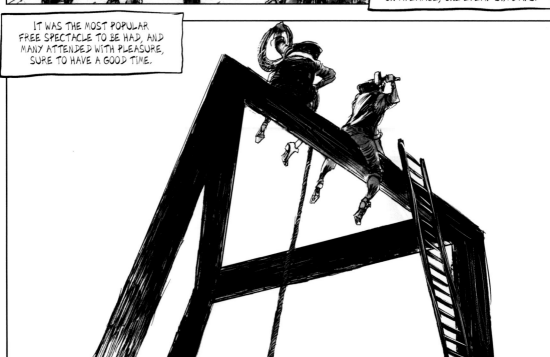

IT WAS THE MOST POPULAR FREE SPECTACLE TO BE HAD, AND MANY ATTENDED WITH PLEASURE, SURE TO HAVE A GOOD TIME.

AND YET IT WAS ORIGINALLY MEANT TO BE A CLEAR DISPLAY OF AN ENDURING PUBLIC AUTHORITY, ANXIOUS TO DEMONSTRATE THE EXEMPLARY OMNIPOTENCE OF ITS SOVEREIGN JUSTICE.

OVER THE YEARS, THE HANGINGS NO LONGER SERVED THEIR PURPOSE. NO ONE WAS COWED. INSTEAD, SOME EVEN DEFIED HIS MAJESTY KING GEORGE THERE, THOUGH HE'D BEEN IN POWER SINCE *1760*.

"YOU, GEORGE SEXTON, DESPITE OUR ACTS OF MERCY TOWARD YOUR PERSON, APPEAR TODAY AS A PRISONER."

YOU KNOW THIS GEORGE SEXTON?

NEVER HEARD OF HIM!

DIDN'T HE KILL ONE OF THE DUKE OF CLARENCE'S SONS?

IN A DUEL?

HE'S A HANDSOME BOY!

HE'S GOT A THIEF'S FACE, NOT A KILLER'S!

"BECAUSE OF YOUR VICE AND IMMORALITY YOU SHALL DIE, AND YOU SHALL HEAR THE BELLS OF SAINT SEPULCHRE, IN THE PARISH OF TYBURN."

THIS BELL TOLLS YOUR TRESPASS, AND THUS WILL GOD'S CREATURES HEAR IT TOO AND PRAY FOR YOU.

LADIES AND GENTS, THANKS FOR COMING! RAISE A GLASS TO MY HEALTH WHEN I'M SWINGING LIFELESS AT THE END OF THIS ROPE!

FOR EVEN AS I'M GONE FROM THIS WORLD, SO SHALL I BE DONE WITH THIS LIFE OF MISERY WHERE WE'VE NO RIGHT TO RUN THROUGH A LORD'S SON THOUGH HE BE AN INCORRIGIBLE SWINDLER!

FAREWELL THEN, I LEAVE HEAD HIGH TO JOIN MY VICTIM, AND INTEND TO KEEP KICKING HIS ARSE...

AND SPITTING ON OUR GOOD KING GEORGE, WHO CARES NOT A WHIT FOR THE POOR AND UNFORTUNATE!

HEAR, HEAR!

WELL SAID, SEXTON!

O YER HEALTH!

EXECUTIONER, DO YOUR DUTY!

NEED I ADD THAT THE 531 EXECUTIONS WERE BUT 46 PER CENT OF THE NUMBER PLANNED?

1,152 CAPITAL SENTENCES HAD BEEN HANDED OUT, BUT THEY WERE COMMUTED TO IMPRISONMENT OR TRANSPORTATION.

EXECUTIONS WERE AN AFFRONT TO ROYAL AUTHORITY AND, ABOVE ALL, LACKED DECENCY.

MEANWHILE THE KING SPORADICALLY EXERCISED HIS PREROGATIVE, THE RIGHT OF PARDON, AND SO GAVE THE IMPRESSION OF BEING MERCIFUL, OF LISTENING TO HIS PEOPLE.

THE RESULT? THERE WERE EVEN MORE PEOPLE IN LONDON'S GAOLS.

WHY DID YOUNG CHILDREN FIND THEMSELVES SWEEPING CHIMNEYS IN LONDON IN 1783?

BECAUSE THEY WERE ORPHANS.

BECAUSE THEY WERE TOO YOUNG TO SAY NO TO ADULTS.

BECAUSE THEY WERE SMALL ENOUGH TO FIT INSIDE CHIMNEYS.

BECAUSE IF THEY DIED AFTERWARDS FROM SUFFOCATION OR INHALING SOOT, NO ONE KNEW.

JOHN KNEW OLD HOLDEN. HE'D ALREADY SWEPT HIS CHIMNEY A FEW MONTHS BEFORE.

BUT NOW IT WAS OCTOBER, AND THE OLD MAN PROBABLY WASN'T RUNNING ANY RISKS WITH THE HARSH WINTER COMING.

HE WAS NICE ENOUGH, A HARMLESS OLD GRANDFATHER...

OF THE KIND JOHN WOULD NEVER HAVE.

IN HIS MEMORY, THE HOUSE WAS COSY, CHARMING, WELCOMING...

THE KIND OF PLACE THAT MADE YOU WANT TO RELAX BY THE FIRE. IT WAS EASY...

SO EASY...

TOO EASY...

JOHN WAS BAFFLED. HE DIDN'T REMEMBER THE ROOM BEING LIKE THIS.

SO YOU COULD HAVE TABLES FOR EATING, ARMCHAIRS FOR SITTING, AND MIRRORS FOR ADMIRING YOURSELF?

OLD MR. HOLDEN MUST'VE BEEN REALLY QUITE RICH.

MADE YOU WONDER IF HE'D NOTICE A WEE SOMETHING GOING MISSING IN ALL THE ABUNDANCE....

AT THAT MOMENT, AS TEMPTATION CROSSED HIS MIND....

JOHN ALSO FELT A TERRIBLE PAIN IN HIS BELLY.

HE HADN'T EATEN FOR THREE DAYS. HE TOTTERED, TRYING TO STAY UPRIGHT.

HE WAS OVERCOME WITH DIZZINESS. HE FELT SICK.

HE TOLD HIMSELF HE WOULDN'T OFTEN GET THE CHANCE TO BE INSIDE SO LUXURIOUS A HOUSE.

IT WAS NOW OR NEVER.

SURELY MR. HOLDEN WOULDN'T NOTICE IF A FEW KNICK-KNACKS WENT MISSING FROM HIS COMMODE?

THAT TYRANT CARTER WOULDN'T KNOW EITHER.

JOHN KNEW OTHER CHILDREN BEFORE HIM HAD USED CHIMNEY SWEEPING TO PILFER VALUABLE OBJECTS TO BRING THEM A FEW SHILLINGS.

NOW IT WAS HIS TURN. AND IF GOD EVER NOTICED WHAT HE DID, HE WOULDN'T BEGRUDGE JOHN'S WANTING TO EAT HIS FILL AND SLEEP UNDER A ROOF... FOR ONCE.

74

A CHILD'S WORLD COMBINES INNOCENCE WITH CRUELTY.

THAT DAY, IN THE MONTH OF OCTOBER 1783, JOHN HUDSON KNEW BOTH.

WHEN YOU'RE NINE YEARS OLD, YOU CAN'T SEE FURTHER AHEAD THAN A FEW HOURS. WHEN HE LEFT OVER THE ROOFTOPS LATER, THAT BORN VAGABOND FELT COMPLETELY INNOCENT.

WHAT'S MORE, HE'D COMPLETELY FORGOTTEN HIS ACTIONS.

JUST AS HE'D FORGOTTEN THE HANGED MAN AT TYBURN.

THOSE WERE ADULT MATTERS. HE WAS TOO YOUNG TO BE BOTHERED WITH THEM.

UH.... MISTER! PLEASE!

WHAT D'YE WANT?

I HAVEN'T EATEN FOR THREE DAYS.

I SAW YOU GIVING YOUR HORSE A CARROT. COULD I HAVE A BIT?

HOW DARE YOU, YOU DIRTY LITTLE BUGGER!

YOU KNOW WHAT A HORSE BRINGS IN, NEXT TO A KID?

JOHN HUDSON! THERE YOU ARE!

BUGGER OFF BEFORE I GET ANGRY!

I'VE BEEN LOOKING FOR YOU FOR AN HOUR! YOU SWEPT MR. HOLDEN'S CHIMNEY LIKE I ASKED, DIDN'T YOU?

UH, YES...

OF COURSE YOU DID.

YOU STILL HAVEN'T GIVEN ME MY COIN.

THE PROBLEM, BOY, IS THAT MR. HOLDEN HERE CAME TO SEE ME IN PERSON.

AND HE WANTS SOME EXPLANATIONS.

HUH?

76

THAT NIGHT, JOHN SLEPT UNDER A ROOF, BUT IT WAS THE ROOF OF A PRISON.

HE WAS IN NEWGATE, WHERE ALL CRIMINALS ENDED UP.

A CURIOUS FATE FOR A BOY WHO'D WOKEN UP IN THE GUTTER THAT MORNING WITH A NOSE FULL OF PISS, TO NOW FIND HIMSELF LOCKED UP THAT NIGHT IN A FILTHY CELL.

SO IT WAS POSSIBLE FOR LIFE TO GET EVEN WORSE....

SILENCE!

CASE OF JOHN HUDSON, FOUND GUILTY OF BURGLARIOUSLY AND FELONIOUSLY BREAKING AND ENTERING.

THE FELONY WAS PERPETRATED ON 17TH OCTOBER LAST, AND TWO OBJECTS OF VALUE WERE TAKEN FROM THE HOUSE OF THE PLAINTIFF, MR. HOLDEN.

TOTAL VALUE: 22 SHILLINGS.

THE ACCUSED WILL COME FORWARD.

HOW OLD ARE YOU?

GOING ON NINE.

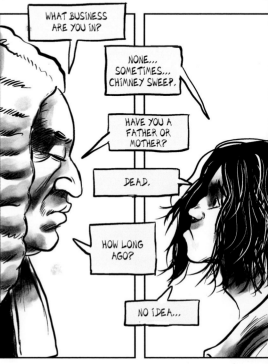

WHAT BUSINESS ARE YOU IN?

NONE... SOMETIMES... CHIMNEY SWEEP.

HAVE YOU A FATHER OR MOTHER?

DEAD.

HOW LONG AGO?

NO IDEA...

EVERYONE THOUGHT THE JUDGE WOULD INSTANTLY DELIVER A STRICT, IF NOT CAPITAL, SENTENCE. THAT WAS WHAT USUALLY HAPPENED.

BUT NOT IN THIS PARTICULAR CASE.

THE JUDGE WAS SEIZED WITH DOUBT.

"I WANTED TO KNOW IF HE UNDERSTOOD THE SITUATION," HE WAS LATER TO CONFIDE.

"I CAN'T ACCEPT THE CONFESSION OF A CHILD OF NINE UNDER SUCH CIRCUMSTANCES, ALL THE MORE TERRIFYING FOR SOMEONE HIS AGE."

"I THINK IT WOULD BE HARSH TO FIND A BOY OF HIS TENDER AGE GUILTY OF THE BURGLARY. HE IS TOO YOUNG FOR THAT. ONLY OF FORCED ENTRY."

"NOR, ON THE OTHER HAND, CAN I FREE HIM. I CANNOT RETURN THIS ORPHAN TO THE STREETS, WHERE HE WILL BE AT THE MERCY OF THE ILL-INTENTIONED."

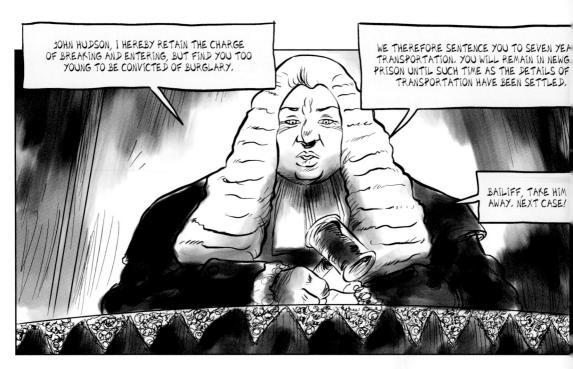

AAARGH...! HUF-HUF....

ARGH... MY GOD....

GOING TO KILL ME, HE IS!

APRIL 1784, LONDON'S EAST END.

HUF-HUF....

THOUGHT YOU'D GET AWAY, EH, MOSELEY?

REALLY THOUGHT YOU'D GET AWAY?

83

THREE MONTHS EARLIER.

END OF THE LINE, BROTHER. LONDON!

"THE SLAVES UNDERSTOOD WAR HAD BROKEN OUT BETWEEN THE PLANTATION OWNERS AND THE ENGLISH. AND THE ENGLISH PROMISED FREEDOM FOR ANYONE WHO'D FIGHT FOR THEM. SO THE SLAVES FLED THE PLANTATIONS..."

"AND WENT TO THE COLONIAL CAPITAL IN WILLIAMSBURG, RUN BY GOVERNOR MURRAY, EARL OF DUNMORE."

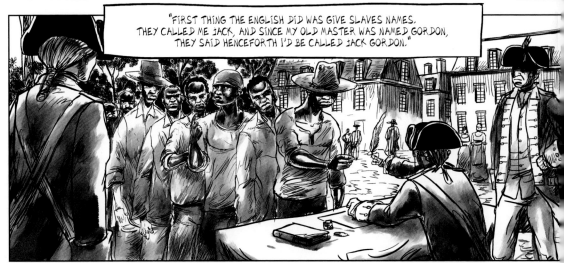

"FIRST THING THE ENGLISH DID WAS GIVE SLAVES NAMES. THEY CALLED ME JACK, AND SINCE MY OLD MASTER WAS NAMED GORDON, THEY SAID HENCEFORTH I'D BE CALLED JACK GORDON."

"AFTERWARDS, THEY GATHERED US TOGETHER AND SAID WE'D HAVE TO FIND THE REBEL COLONISTS."

"SEEMS THEY WANTED TO REVOLT AND DRIVE OUT THE ENGLISH TO MAKE THE UNITED STATES OF AMERICA! EVEN THOUGH THEY USED TO BE ENGLISH THEMSELVES."

"WE DIDN'T UNDERSTAND NOTHIN' ABOUT IT ALL, EXCEPTIN' THAT WE MIGHT LOSE OUR HIDES."

"WHICH HAPPENED TO A LOT OF OUR BROTHERS. WE WENT FROM THE TOBACCO FIELDS TO THE BATTLEFIELDS, AND BOY, WERE THOSE WORSE!"

"AFTER INDEPENDENCE WAS DECLARED,
WE FOUND OURSELVES IN NEW YORK,
WHICH THE ENGLISH STILL HELD."

"WE LIVED IN AN ARMY CAMP ON THE EAST RIVER THERE, BY BROOKLYN.
LOTS OF BLACK FOLK WORKING FOR THE WAGON MASTER GENERAL, MAKING STREETS
AND ROADS. I TOOK THE CHANCE TO CHANGE MY NAME; NOW I'M DANIEL GORDON.
LIKED IT BETTER. FELT LIKE I WAS FREED ALL OVER..."

"THEN WHEN THE AMERICANS REACHED NEW YORK,
THE ENGLISH EVACUATED US OFF TO ENGLAND..."

WE LIVED IN SQUALOR IN NEW YORK, WE'LL LIVE IN SQUALOR IN LONDON.

MAKES SENSE, RIGHT? BLACK MAN, FORMER SLAVE — YOU THINK WE'D REALLY HAVE A SHOT AT MAKING IT?

ALL THESE CHILDREN...

LIKELY ALL ORPHANS, ABANDONED.

GONNA BE TOUGH, CAESAR!

AT LEAST YOU'RE BIG AND STRONG. LUCKY! ME, I...

HEY! DANIEL GORDON! IS THAT YOU?

WILLIAM BLUE! CAN IT BE? LAST TIME I SAW YOU, YOU WERE SINGING IN A BROOKLYN BASEMENT.

AND YOU'RE STILL SMOKING THAT OLD PIPE! HOW ARE YOU, MY BROTHER!

MAY I INTRODUCE CAESAR, THE MOST STRAPPING LAD I KNOW!

BIG CRITTER, AIN'T HE?

THIS IS WHERE WE SLEEP. DON'T ASK FOR MORE, OR BETTER... THIS IS IT!

SIXPENCE A NIGHT TO THE OWNER. TEN'LL FIT NO PROBLEM.

IF YOU SHOW UP AT THE BOARD OF LOYALISTS, YOU CAN GET SOME MONEY!

EH? YOU MEAN WE GET WAGES?

OF COURSE! YOU FOUGHT FOR THE REDCOATS DURING THE WAR, AND GOT EVACUATED FROM NEW YORK WHEN THE YANKEES CAME? THEN YOU'VE A RIGHT TO WAGES.

WELL, DON'T THAT BEAT ALL! AND CAESAR?

HE'LL GET CIVILIAN WORKERS' WAGES.

"LOOKS LIKE WE COULD DO WORSE THAN LIVING IN LONDON..."

"WE BLACKS, FORMER SLAVES, THE FORGOTTEN MEN OF REVOLUTIONS, GHOSTS OF THE WESTERN CAPITALS..."

"FOR US, NIGHT SHOULD BE OUR SACRED REFUGE, OUR TERRITORY, OUR PRESERVE..."

"SOMEDAY I, CAESAR, WILL BE FREE, AND IN THE DARK HOURS I WILL WALK IN GREAT WOODS THAT WILL WELCOME ME LIKE A NOMAD AND MAN BLESSED."

"SOMEDAY I WILL NO LONGER SEE EVIL EVERYWHERE, FOR I WILL BE AT PEACE. I WILL HAVE COME TO MY JOURNEY'S END, AND I WILL KNOW IT IS TIME TO LIVE AT LAST, RATHER THAN WATCH OTHERS RUTTING."

"AND YOU SAY YOUR NAME IS...?"

CAESAR. SOMETIMES BLACK CAESAR, TOO.

WE MET ON THE BOAT FROM NEW YORK.

I GUARANTEE HE'S BEEN SERVING HIS MAJESTY FOR AT LEAST TWO YEARS.

THE PROBLEM IS, I HAVE "CAESAR" ON MY LIST, BUT HE'S ALREADY COME FOR HIS BACK PAY.

WHAT'S THIS BUSINESS? I CAME TO LONDON TWO DAYS AGO, AND THIS IS MY FIRST TIME HERE!

SEE FOR YOURSELF! THIS CROSS BESIDE THE NAME "CAESAR"...

INDICATES BEYOND DOUBT THAT SOMEONE HAS ALREADY CLAIMED YOUR MONEY.

TAKE A GOOD LOOK AT ME! DO YOU THINK THERE ARE TWO OF ME? THERE WAS ONLY EVER ONE CAESAR IN NEW YORK!

WELL, HOW WOULD I KNOW? YOU NEGROES HAVE NO PAPERS, AND YOU ALL LOOK ALIKE! SOMEONE MUST HAVE HOODWINKED YOU, CHUM!

IF I EVER GET A HOLD OF THAT BASTARD...

The Three Cats

STEALING FROM A BROTHER IS THE WORST CRIME. BESIDES, IT MUST BE SOMEONE WHO KNOWS ME, AND KNEW I WASN'T IN LONDON YET.

YOU MUST HAVE MET IN NEW YORK, BUT HE GOT HERE BEFORE YOU.

DON'T WORRY, CAESAR. WE GOT OUR MONEY. WE CAN HELP YOU OUT FOR NOW.

THANK YOU, DANIEL. I EXPECTED NO LESS. BUT I STILL WANT TO FIND THAT BASTARD!

CAESAR! HOW GOES IT? THERE'S A PUBLIC EXECUTION IN KENNINGTON TOMORROW. COMING WITH?

HELLO, MO. DON'T KNOW. I'LL SEE.

YOU'RE VERY POPULAR ALREADY, CAESAR, AND YOUR STATURE COMMANDS RESPECT. YOU'RE IN LUCK.

LUCK? HAVEN'T HAD MUCH OF THAT LATELY.

96

EVENING, JOHN.

SEE YOU TOMORROW, SIR.

YOU ALL ALONE, GUV'NOR? WANT TO STICK YOUR DICK UP A NICE WARM MUFF AND HAVE A GOOD TIME?

HELLO.

98

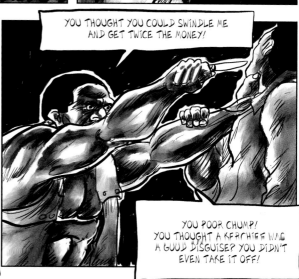

SILENCE!

JOHN MOSELEY, YOU ARE SENTENCED TO DEATH FOR FRAUDULENT IDENTITY AND USURPING ANOTHER MAN'S PAY! PENDING YOUR EXECUTION, YOU WILL REMAIN IN NEWGATE PRISON!

BRAM!

SUMMER, 1784 A.D.
A MAN CLIMBS A STEEP, CRAGGY PATH BY THE SEA.

ARTHUR PHILLIP.

ENGLISH.
46.
OLD.
ALONE.

HE WATCHES HIS STEP, FAR FROM BOLD —
NAY, SLOW, SOBER, TROUBLED. FIRST TIME IN FRANCE.

HE'S DOUBTING AND QUESTIONING.

HE IS DEEPLY TROUBLED.

IT'S A HOT AFTERNOON:
A DRY, STIFLING HEAT.

SO DIFFERENT FROM THE HUMID
WINDS HE FELT IN OTHER LANDS,
YEARS BEFORE.

HERE, IN THE SOUTHWEST
OF FRANCE, ONE MUST FIRST OF
ALL ACCEPT THE SOUND OF CICADAS,
WHICH NO ONE DISTURBS.

THE PEOPLE HERE STAY HOME
IN WEATHER LIKE THIS, AND IF YOU
ASK THEM WHY, THEY'LL SAY IT'S
SIESTA TIME.

WHO'D CONTRADICT THEM?

AND SO NO ONE BOTHERS THE OLD
ENGLISHMAN WHO HAS DECIDED TO
BRAVE THE SUN AND QUICKLY FULFIL
THE MISSION HE WAS SENT ON.

105

FOR ONCE, THE ENGLISH AND THE FRENCH ARE NOT OFFICIALLY AT WAR. BUT THEY PROBABLY WILL BE AGAIN SOMEDAY SOON.

WHICH IS WHY PRECAUTIONS MUST BE TAKEN. CAN'T MISS A CHANCE TO CHECK UP ON THE STATE OF THE FRENCH NAVY.

TO RULE THE SEAS IS TO RULE THE WORLD, ISN'T IT? NO HARM IN BEING A TOURIST AND A SPY AT THE SAME TIME.

ARTHUR PHILLIP KNOWS WHY HE IS NOT THE ONLY SPECIAL ENVOY THE HOME OFFICE OF HIS MOST GRACIOUS MAJESTY KING GEORGE III HAS SENT TO THE LAND OF HIS GREAT RIVAL LOUIS XVI.

HE SUSPECTS HIS FRIEND EVAN NEPEAN — MORE A CONTACT, REALLY, AND THE POWER BEHIND THE THRONE OF THE HOME SECRETARY, LORD SYDNEY — OF HAVING ARRANGED THIS MISSION TO GIVE HIM SOMETHING UNDEMANDING TO DO.

FOR CAPTAIN ARTHUR PHILLIP, R.N., HAS NO PROSPECT OF A NAVAL COMMAND. NOR HAS HE ANY ILLUSIONS ABOUT THE FATE OF HIS REPORT. ANOTHER SHEET OF PAPER IN THE ARCHIVES, AN ANONYMOUS DOCUMENT.

ANONYMITY... YES, THAT'S HIS PRIMARY QUALITY.

HOW CAN SOMEONE BORN IN ENGLAND TO A GERMAN FATHER HOPE TO LEAVE HIS MARK ON HISTORY?

AN ADMIRABLE MAN, JAKOB PHILLIP, ORIGINALLY FROM FRANKFURT, WHO RATHER INOPPORTUNELY PASSED AWAY WHILE ARTHUR AND HIS SISTER WERE STILL YOUNG...

LEAVING BEHIND A MOTHER, ALREADY WIDOWED ONCE BY A NAVAL OFFICER, PENNILESS AND WITHOUT PROSPECTS FOR HER ELDEST SON.

HAPPILY, MRS. PHILLIP HAS COMMON SENSE. SHE REMEMBERS THAT HER FIRST HUSBAND'S FRIENDS SHOWED UP AT HIS FUNERAL...

...VOWING HELP AND SUPPORT IF NEEDED.

AND THAT IS HOW, AT 13, YOUNG ARTHUR...

FINDS HIMSELF A BOARDER AT THE ROYAL HOSPITAL SCHOOL...

IN GREENWICH.

TWO YEARS LATER THE YOUNG MAN IS AN APPRENTICE ON THE *FORTUNE*, A WHALER PATROLLING THE ARCTIC IN SEARCH OF PRECIOUS MEAT.

A TRAUMATIZING EXPERIENCE.

FIRSTLY BECAUSE IT IS IN THE MERCHANT NAVY, WHEN MANY OF HIS MORE FORTUNATE OR ENTERPRISING PEERS...

HAVE BEEN POSTED TO THE NAVY AND ITS GREAT MEN-OF-WAR.

SECONDLY, BECAUSE THE GLACIAL TEMPERATURES PIERCE THE VERY DEPTHS OF HIS YOUNG APPRENTICE SOUL.

SUCH COLD IS INHUMAN. IT MAKES YOU WANT TO SCREAM, JUMP OVERBOARD.

BUT ARTHUR PHILLIP MAKES NOT A SOUND.

HE ENDURES. HE SUFFERS. HE GROWS FRAGILE AND SICKLY, BUT REMAINS SILENT.

THIS TERRIBLE TRIAL IS NO DOUBT THE WAY TO HIS FUTURE. HIS DESTINY.

HE CONSOLES HIMSELF WITH THIS THOUGHT: AFTER SUCH A HARSH INITIATION TO NAVAL LIFE, HE CAN FACE ANYTHING.

NOW IT IS 1756.

AFTER ENTERING THE ROYAL NAVY, ARTHUR PHILLIP IS A MIDSHIPMAN CADET.

ABOARD THE *BUCKINGHAM*, A 68-GUN SHIP COMMANDED BY CAPTAIN EVERITT, A DISTANT COUSIN OF HIS MOTHER'S.

MAY 20TH THAT YEAR SEES HIS BAPTISM BY FIRE. ENGLAND AND FRANCE WERE AT WAR AGAIN, AND IT WOULD LAST SEVEN YEARS.

BUT FOR NOW — JUST A BRIEF SKIRMISH IN THE MEDITERRANEAN, NEAR MINORCA.

THE *BUCKINGHAM* IS BATTLING *LE SAGE* AND THE DAMNED FRENCH HAVE THE ADVANTAGE.

THE REINFORCEMENTS NEVER CAME: JOHN BYNG, ADMIRAL OF THE FLEET, DECIDED TO FALL BACK TOWARDS GIBRALTAR.

IT IS A MIRACLE THE *BUCKINGHAM* ESCAPES INTACT.

AND A COURT MARTIAL AWAITS BYNG.

TWO MONTHS LATER, THE ADMIRAL IS EXECUTED ABOARD A SHIP ANCHORED AT PORTSMOUTH. IN 1759, VOLTAIRE USED THE EPISODE IN *CANDIDE*: "IN THIS COUNTRY IT IS FOUND GOOD, FROM TIME TO TIME, TO KILL ONE ADMIRAL TO ENCOURAGE THE OTHERS."

THE BATTLE OF MINORCA HAS MENTAL AND PHYSICAL CONSEQUENCES.

AT THE AGE OF 18, ARTHUR PHILLIP IS RELIEVED OF DUTY.

IT IS AS IF THE GLACIERS FROM THREE YEARS BEFORE ARE EATING AWAY AT HIS MIND AND BODY.

HE KEEPS COUGHING, HE IS ALWAYS COLD AND WEAK. HE GROWS FRAIL.

HE HAS NO PAY, AND HIS MOTHER CAN DO NOTHING FOR HIM.

HE REMAINS ILL FOR THREE YEARS.

HE BEGINS TO IMPROVE. HIS MOTHER'S FRIENDS REMEMBER HIM AND TAKE PITY.

IN 1760, AT THE AGE OF 22, HE JOINS THE STIRLING CASTLE AS A MERE SEAMAN.

HE SAILS TO INDIA. THE CLIMATE THERE IS BETTER FOR HIM.

HE COMES INTO HIS OWN. OTHERS NOTICE.

HE IS MADE A SUB-LIEUTENANT.

HE TAKES PART IN THE SIEGE OF HAVANA AGAINST THE SPANISH.

THE ENGLISH WIN.

HE IS PAID AS A RESULT. HE GOES HOME AND ENJOYS LIFE.

HE TAKES A BREAK FROM HIS MEMORIES. HE'S RIGHT IN THE SUN. IT'S TOO HOT.

WHERE WAS HE?

HE'S 24.
HE MEETS MARGARET DENISON, WHOM EVERYONE CALLS CHARLOTTE.

SHE IS 41.

SHE FANCIES THE KIND, DISCREET, AND OBLIGING YOUNG MAN. HE SEES A HEART MORE SOLITARY THAN HIS OWN.

THEY ARE MARRIED IN 1763.

ARTHUR SIGNS A PROMISE TO LAY NO CLAIM TO HER FORTUNE OR EXTENSIVE LANDS.

THEY MAKE THEIR HOME IN DEVON, AND ARTHUR, WHO ENTERTAINS IDEAS OF CHANGING PROFESSIONS, BECOMES A FARMER. IT KEEPS HIM BUSY, BUT DOESN'T EXCITE HIM.

CHARLOTTE GROWS BORED.

HIS FIELDS AND MARRIAGE HAVE THIS MUCH IN COMMON: THEY RUN FALLOW.

THE COUPLE GROW APART, GO SEPARATE WAYS.

THE DIVORCE IN 1769 IS A MERE FORMALITY.

1774. ARTHUR GETS BACK IN TOUCH WITH THE *STIRLING CASTLE'S* FORMER CAPTAIN, WHO HAS SINCE BECOME A MEMBER OF THE ADMIRALTY BOARD.

HE, AT LEAST, HASN'T WASTED THE LAST FOURTEEN YEARS.

AUGUSTUS HERVEY — FOR THAT IS HIS NAME — RECOMMENDS HIM TO THE PORTUGUESE AMBASSADOR IN LONDON.

THIS ALLY IS IN FACT LOOKING FOR NAVAL OFFICERS FOR ITS ENDLESS STRUGGL WITH THE SPANIARDS OFF THE COAST OF SOUTH AMERICA.

A DEAL IS MADE: FROM A MERE 2ND LIEUTENANT IN THE NAVY, ARTHUR SUDDENLY BECOMES A CAPTAIN FOR THE PORTUGUESE. SOON HE IS THE MASTER, NEXT AFTER GOD, OF HIS OWN SHIP: *NOSSA SENHORA DO PILAR.*

THAT'S THIRTEEN YEARS HE'S RECLAIMED, GIVEN THE USUA CRAWL UP THE ENGLISH RANKS.

IN 1777, HE WINS A DECISIVE VICTORY AGAINST THE SPANIARDS OFF RIO. THE COLONIAL GOVERNOR SINGS HIS PRAISES.

COULD BE USEFUL SOMEDAY, ARTHUR THINKS. YOU NEVER KNOW.

112

HE RETURNS TO ENGLAND. IT IS NEVER GOOD TO STAY AWAY TOO LONG FROM THE ADMIRALTY, WHERE EVERYTHING HAPPENS.

HE IS RETURNED TO THE RANK OF 2ND LIEUTENANT — AT 41! — AND SHIPPED OUT ON THE *ALEXANDER*, PATROLLING THE CHANNEL, KEEPING EYE ON ANY FRENCH MOVEMENTS.

SELFLESSNESS BRINGS ITS REWARD. HE IS FINALLY MADE CAPTAIN, AND GIVEN COMMAND OF THE *BASILISK*.

THEN THE *VICTORY*!

THERE HE MAKES THE ACQUAINTANCE OF A YOUNG CIVIL SERVANT: AMBITIOUS, WITH SOLID CONNECTIONS AND HIS SIGHTS SET ON AN IMPORTANT POST IN A MINISTRY.

HIS NAME IS EVAN NEPEAN. HE ENJOYS PHILLIP'S COMPANY, HIS POLYGLOT TALENTS.

AND THINKS: HOW RARE, AN OFFICER WITHOUT FAMILIAL TIES ON DRY LAND...

YEARS GO BY. NOT MUCH CHANGES.
KEEPING AN EYE ON THE CHANNEL, MOSTLY;
SOMETIMES THE MEDITERRANEAN.

OFF THE COAST OF RIO AGAIN.
ARTHUR CAPTAINS THE *EUROPE*, A 64-GUN
BOAT SENT TO SPY ON SPANISH POSITIONS NEAR
THE ESTUARY OF THE RIO DE LA PLATA.

ONE DAY, A PORTUGUESE FORT
FIRES ON HIM. HOW DARE IT!

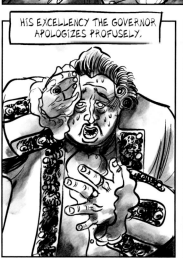
HIS EXCELLENCY THE GOVERNOR
APOLOGIZES PROFUSELY.

"YOU ARE ALWAYS
WELCOME IN RIO," HE
ASSURES THEM.

HIS MISSION IS OVER, AT ANY RATE. HE RETURNS
TO LONDON TO FIND NEPEAN UNDER-SECRETARY
OF STATE FOR THE HOME OFFICE.

HE HAS NO POSTING. NEPEAN
GIVES HIM A NEW SPY MISSION
TO FRANCE.

ARTHUR PHILLIP IS SWEATING.
HE SEES HIS LIFE FLASH BY IN A
FEW SECONDS, AND WONDERS IF IT
AMOUNTS TO ANYTHING.

HE HAS NEVER MADE A GLARING ERROR,
AND IN A FEW YEARS WILL MAKE ADMIRAL,
THE REWARD FOR A SAILOR'S LIFE.

AN ADMIRAL FROM SENIORITY
AND NOT MERIT.

AN ADMIRAL WHOSE LIFE WILL
LEAVE NO TRACE AMONG HIS PEERS.

HE HEADS BACK DOWN THE
PATH, CAREFULLY NOTING WHAT
HE HAS SEEN IN TOULON.

THE FRENCH MAINTAIN THEIR
FLEET UNENTHUSIASTICALLY,
NO MILITARY MANOEUVRES
IN SIGHT.

SUDDENLY IT SEEMS AN OBVIOUS ANALOGY
FOR HIS OWN CAREER, DEFINITIVELY
DISMAL AND DREARY.

WITH A HEAVY STEP, HE WALKS OFF, HEAD BOWED.
46 YEARS OF LONELINESS ARE SLOWLY DYING IN THE
SHADOW HE CASTS ON THE PATH.

HIS LIFE, DEVOID OF MYSTERY,
NEEDS NO COMMENT.

WHEN NEWGATE PRISON A FEW YEARS AGO
A FIRE DID CONSUME, THEY CRIED:

O WOE!

ALL THOSE PRISONERS HAD TO BE HOUSED SOMEWHERE.
REBUILD THEY DID, SO GRAND THAT SOME WOULD SWEAR
THE PRISON WAS ITSELF A CITADEL, ITS MASSIVE DOORS
THE LOST SOUL'S GATE TO HELL.

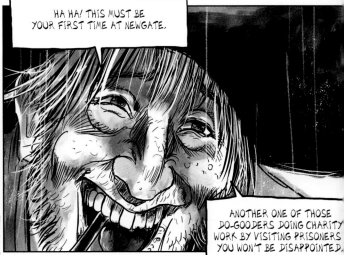

119

BLOODY VERMIN!

SPEAKING OF WHICH...

WHAT ARE YOU DOING HERE?

ME? UH, NOTHING!

I'VE SEEN YOU BEFORE.

YOU'RE JOHN HUDSON, RIGHT?

HOW OLD ARE YOU?

12. I THINK...

IF YOU'RE HERE AT 12, YOU MUST'VE STOLEN SOMETHING, RIGHT?

ANYONE TELL YOU WHY I'M HERE?

NO.

MAYBE THAT'S FOR THE BEST, LITTLE MAN.

LOOK: TODAY'S VISITORS HAVE ARRIVED. YOU EXPECTING ANYONE?

NO, I'M AN ORPHAN.

HOW LONG ARE YOU IN FOR?

ME? UN THEY H ME.

AND YOU?

SEVEN YEARS' TRANSPORTATION.

I'VE BEEN HERE A YEAR. I'M COUNTING THE DAYS.

AWFUL. AT YOUR AGE, YOU SLEEP WELL AT NIGHT?

NO.

OF COURSE NOT...

WHAT WITH THE SCREAMS OF THE MAD AND THE BUGGERED...

THE GUARDS AND THEIR BOOZE, AND COLD CLUTCHING AT YOUR GUTS.

WHAT YOU NEED IN SUCH A HOSTILE ENVIRONMENT IS A LITTLE MORE SAFETY.

HOW'S THAT?

I DON'T KNOW... SOME KIND OF PROTECTOR. A BIG BROTHER, ALMOST. TO WATCH OUT FOR YOU.

DON'T KNOW...

YES YOU DO, JOHN.

I COULD BE HIM! AND I WILL BE.

BUT HOW?

I SAID I'D WATCH OUT FOR YOU, JOHN. IN EXCHANGE—

IN EXCHANGE?

I'LL EXPLAIN. COME WITH ME.

WHERE ARE WE GOING?

DON'T WORRY. A QUIET SPOT.

I'D LIKE YOU TO LEAVE ME ALONE, SIR.

SIR? THAT'S A BIT MUCH.

I'M NO NOBLEMAN, MY BOY. I'M A REGULAR BLOKE LIKE YOURSELF.

A NOBODY ALL THE TO...

EXCE... I WI... YO... WEL...

LET ME GO! I'M FINE ON MY OWN!

YOU POOR FOOL, THERE ARE SICK, TWISTED MEN HERE! WHAT WILL YOU DO? COME WITH ME, I SAY!

AAARRGH!

UF.... HUF....

THERE YOU ARE!

YOU'D BEST STOP RIGHT NOW, OR I'LL—

AAAAA

WANT TO KNOW WHY I WAS SENT HERE?

131

132

PRAK!

PRAK!
PRAK!
PRAK!

WHOMP!
WHOMP!

DON'T HURT ME, CAESAR...

WHAT'S THAT SMELL?

IS THAT YOU?

I COULDN'T HELP MYSELF.

I'M.... SORRY, CAESAR.

JUST BECAUSE YOU SMELL LIKE SHIT DON'T MEAN YOU HAVE TO WALLOW IN IT.

DON'T WORRY. EVERYTHING HERE STINKS ANYWAY. NO ONE WILL BLAME YOU.

I DON'T HAVE OTHER CLOTHES.

NO SURPRISE, ME NEITHER. BUT WE CAN FIX THAT.

WHEN HE WAKES UP, HE'S GONNA KILL ME.

NOT FROM NOW ON, STAY WITH ME, I'LL PROTECT YOU. CAESAR'S WORD.

DON'T LET THEM GIVE YOU SHIT IN THIS BLOODY LIFE, OTHERWISE YOU'RE FUCKED.

135

"JOHN, LET ME INTRODUCE YOUR NEW FRIENDS. A BIT CRAMPED HERE, BUT IT WORKS OUT."

"THIS IS JOHN MOSELEY. WE HAD A LITTLE DIFFERENCE OF OPINION IN THE PAST, BUT WE BOTH WOUND UP HERE."

"NOW WE HELP EACH OTHER OUT. WE'RE IN THE SAME BOAT."

WHAT HAPPENED?

THAT NITWIT STOLE MY PAY. I NABBED HIM AND TURNED HIM IN. THEN I STOLE MONEY MYSELF. SEVEN YEARS' TRANSPORTATION, HELLO NEWGATE!

I'M SENTENCED TO HANG. YOU'LL OUTLIVE ME, CAESAR!

I HEARD EXECUTIONS WERE OVER. THEY'RE GOING TO EXILE US INSTEAD.

I HEAR KING GEORGE WANTS HIS AMERICAN COLONIES BACK, BUT HE CAN SHOVE THEM UP HIS ASS!

I'M NEVER GOING BACK TO THOSE SLAVER

ANYWAY, THIS IS JANE. WE HAD A KID TOGETHER. TRYING TO GET PARDONED IF GEORGE WILL ALLOW IT.

YOU THINK WE'LL REALLY GET OUT OF HERE SOMEDAY?

WE'RE NOT TREATED LIKE HUMANS HERE. A KID LIKE YOU, JOHN, SHOULDN'T BE LOCKED UP WITH ALL THESE FREAKS — I MEAN THE PRISONERS AND THE GUARDS!

I DON'T KNOW IF IT'LL BE ANY BETTER, JOHN, GOING TO DIE IN SOME DESERT. DON'T SEE THE POINT.

WE DON'T HAVE MUCH HOPE, THAT'S FOR SURE.

I THINK I KNOW WHAT HAPPENED TO YOU TODAY, JOHN. I SAW YOU EARLIER, WHEN THAT ABOMINATION TERRY MILES, THE CHILD RAPIST, WAS CHASING YOU.

THANKS...

DON'T WORRY, SON. STAY WITH US, AND CAESAR WILL WATCH OVER YOU. C'MON, SIT DOWN.

YOU DESERVE TO BE GUTTED AND LEFT TO BLEED OUT LIKE A STUCK PIG!

LET ME TELL YOU, CAESAR: NEGROES DON'T MAKE THE LAWS HERE!

I'LL TAKE CARE OF YOU SOON ENOUGH! YOU CAN BET YOU'LL BE SHIPPED OUT ON A HULK!

YOU'LL FIT IN OUT THERE, WITH THE SEASICK AND THE MADDEST PRISONERS OF ALL.

THAT'S WHY WE TOSS THEM TO THE WAVES!

MEANWHILE, A LITTLE PUNISHMENT: 150 LASHES!

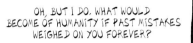

OH, BUT I DO. WHAT WOULD BECOME OF HUMANITY IF PAST MISTAKES WEIGHED ON YOU FOREVER?

AND?

I HAVE GIVEN YOUR PROPOSITION SOME THOUGHT.

YOU PROPOSE TO FOUND A COLONY IN NEW SOUTH WALES WHICH, AND I QUOTE:

"IS A LAND MOST APTLY SUITED TO THE PROPENSITIES OF EUROPEAN ADVENTURERS."

WHAT, SPECIFICALLY, DID YOU HAVE IN MIND?

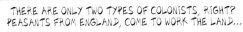

THERE ARE ONLY TWO TYPES OF COLONISTS, RIGHT? PEASANTS FROM ENGLAND, COME TO WORK THE LAND...

...AND AMERICAN LOYALISTS LIKE ME WHO, DISPOSSESSED OF MOST OF THEIR PROPERTY AND THEIR ALLEGIANCE TO THE CROWN, ARE SEEKING NEW REFUGE.

YOU ALSO MENTION THE PINE WOODS AND THAT PLANT... FLAX, IS IT?

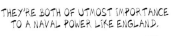

THEY'RE BOTH OF UTMOST IMPORTANCE TO A NAVAL POWER LIKE ENGLAND.

PINE IS THE STURDIEST WOOD FOR MAKING MASTS, AND THE QUANTITIES OVER THERE ARE INFINITE!

AS FOR FLAX, THE POTENTIAL USES FOR ITS FIBRES ARE VAST!

YOU'VE THOUGHT OF EVERYTHING.

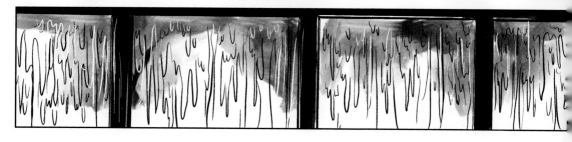

"AH, THE SUN'S OUT AGAIN. WONDERFUL!"

"WE WERE STARTING TO DESPAIR OF EVER SEEING IT AGAIN THIS SEASON, USUALLY THE SUNNIEST!"

"BUT FORGIVE ME, DEAR EVAN, I INTERRUPTED YOU. YOU WERE SAYING?"

I WAS SAYING THIS MATRA IS CLEARLY A TOTAL IDIOT, AS COOK COULD TELL, BUT NOT COMPLETELY WITHOUT IDEAS.

I DID SOME RESEARCH: HE IS CURRENTLY WITHOUT GAINFUL EMPLOY, BUT WITH EVERY MEANS AVAILABLE....

USES HIS PARTICIPATION IN THE *ENDEAVOUR'S* EXPEDITION TO FLATTER HIS AFFAIRS.

IN SHORT: HE'S IN IT FOR THE MONEY.

HOW'S THAT?

DON'T YOU SEE WHERE I'M GOING?

NOW WAIT... YOU'RE SUGGESTING THAT—

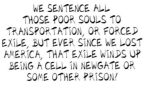

WE SENTENCE ALL THOSE POOR SOULS TO TRANSPORTATION, OR FORCED EXILE, BUT EVER SINCE WE LOST AMERICA, THAT EXILE WINDS UP BEING A CELL IN NEWGATE OR SOME OTHER PRISON!

LET US MAKE GOOD THE SENTENCE AGAIN, AND MAKE THEM COLONISTS! IN BOTANY BAY OR ELSEWHERE!

A NEW TERRITORY TO RID OURSELVES OF OUR CRIMINALS?

HMM, LET'S SAY RATHER A COLONY TO EASE CONGESTION IN THE GAOLS AND REASSURE THE PUBLIC...

YES, YES, I'LL SPEAK TO THE PRIME MINISTER ABOUT IT. DRAFT ME A QUICK WORD THAT SUMS UP YOUR POSITION, WILL YOU?

OF COURSE, SIR.

"MEANWHILE, LET US ENJOY THIS BEAUTIFUL DAY."

I DON'T UNDERSTAND. WE RESTORED QUITE A NUMBER OF HULKS.

YES, SIR, BUT NOT ENOUGH.

YOU'RE TELLING ME THAT THERE'S A THOUSAND MORE PRISONERS EVERY YEAR?

THOSE ARE THE FIGURES FROM MY DEPARTMENT. IN OTHER WORDS, WE'RE PAST OVERCROWDING.

NOT TO MENTION THE DEPLORABLE SANITARY CONDITIONS AND GENERAL RISKS OF INFECTION IN LONDON. WE'RE CAUGHT BETWEEN THE UNSAFE AND THE INSALUBRIOUS!

IF I UNDERSTAND YOU RIGHTLY, THE ONLY PROBLEM IS ITS LOCATION?

YES. IN THEORY, I AM IN FAVOUR OF A SPECIAL FLEET TO A NEW TERRITORY, BUT WE MUST ACT QUICKLY, AND I MUST FIRST SPEAK TO THE KING.

HE'LL BE DELIGHTED TO FOUND A NEW COLONY!

I AGREE. HE STILL HASN'T STOMACHED THE LOSS OF THE AMERICAN TERRITORIES, BUT HE WON'T AGREE TO JUST ANY PRICE.

"AT ANY RATE, IN TERMS OF ORGANIZATION AND SECURITY ON SUCH A JOURNEY, WE ARE FACING AN URGENT SITUATION."

"TIME IS CLEARLY RUNNING SHORT."

WINTER WILL BE HERE SOON, LORD SYDNEY. WE MUST PREPARE FOR THE VOYAGE POST HASTE!

I AM WELL AWARE OF IT. NEPEAN IS WORKING DAY AND NIGHT.

WE MUST STRIKE A BLOW FOR PUBLIC OPINION! WHAT WITH HUNDREDS OF FORCED RECRUITS SENT INTO EXILE, AND AS MANY SOLDIERS AND SAILORS AGAIN.

WE'VE ALREADY TRANSFERRED ALL THE CONVICTS CONCERNED — MORE THAN 700! — ONTO THE SHIPS AT PORTSMOUTH.

WE STILL NEED TO FIND SOMEONE TO COMMAND THE FLEET. I UNDERSTAND THE ADMIRALTY IS DRAGGING ITS FEET.

BUT WITH THE POST OF COLONIAL GOVERNOR AT STAKE, IT SHOULDN'T BE TOO DIFFICULT!

LET'S HOPE SO, SIR...

HOW GOES IT WITH THE SHIPS?

I'VE CALLED ON A SHIPOWNER IN WALWORTH WHO HAS ALREADY READIED THREE SHIPS FOR FOOD AND SUPPLIES.

THE PRISONERS SHOULD BE KEPT IN SIX SHIPS, AS WELL AS ONE OR TWO GUNNERS AND A FLAGSHIP.

TEN VESSELS IN TOTAL, SO...

BUT THIS IS A VERITABLE ARMADA!

WITH THE SOLDIERS AND SAILORS, IT COMES TO MORE THAN 7,000 PEOPLE TO TRANSPORT 15,000 MILES AWAY. IT WILL BE COSTLY. QUITE COSTLY.

GOOD LORD... AND NO ONE WANTS TO CAPTAIN IT, I PRESUME?

THE OFFICERS WILL BE AS MUCH EXILES AS THE PRISONERS, AND RETURN IS NOT NECESSARILY GUARANTEED

AT BEST, THE MISSION RESEMBLES A ROAD TO NOWHERE, AT WORST A TRAP. BUT I HAVE AN IDEA...

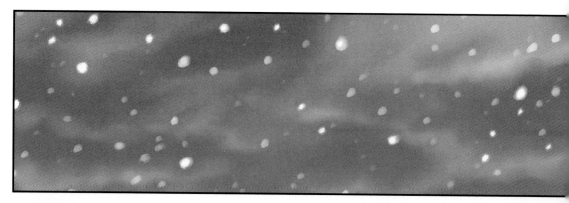

AFTER HIS TIME IN NEWGATE, JOHN HUDSON HAD BEEN TRANSFERRED TO H.M.S. DUNKIRK OFF THE COAST OF PORTSMOUTH.

TWO AND A HALF YEARS LATER, HE WAS STILL THERE.

EVERY DAY HE LABOURED, BUILDING DYKES AROUND THE PORT.

THAT DAY, DESPITE THE SEA AND THE WIND, IT WAS SNOWING IN PORTSMOUTH.

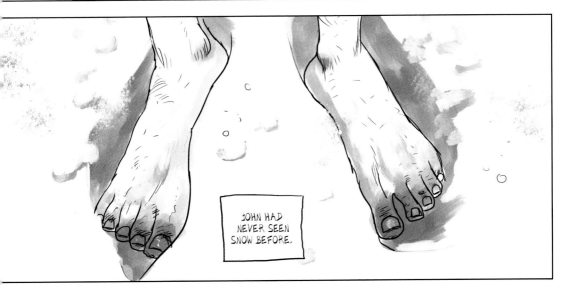

JOHN HAD NEVER SEEN SNOW BEFORE.

DARK, BEACHED CARCASSES, THE PRISON HULKS WERE LIKE THE GATES OF HELL. ABANDON HOPE, ALL YE WHO ENTER HERE. THERE WOULD BE NO SALVATION WITHIN.

THEY HAD TOLD JOHN HE WOULD SOON BE TRANSFERRED AGAIN, LIKE THE OTHER PRISONERS, ON TO A BOAT — A REAL ONE! — LEAVING FOR BOTANY BAY, WHERE HE WOULD SERVE OUT HIS TIME.

BOTANY BAY? HE'D NEVER HEARD OF IT BEFORE, AND HAD NO IDEA WHERE IT WAS.

159

160

PUTTING US IN GAOL OR ON HULKS FOR STEALING TUPPENCE OR A HANDKERCHIEF...

MAKING US WORK OUTSIDE IN ALL WEATHER AND NOT CARING IF WE DIE — THAT'S GOD'S INJUSTICE, JOHN!

BUT PUNISHING A MAN WHEN HE'S DONE NO WRONG — THAT'S MAN'S INJUSTICE.

"YOU'VE SEEN BOTH AT WORK TODAY."

"THEY'RE MAKING CAESAR A WOUNDED ANIMAL — THE MOST DANGEROUS KIND!"

BUT WE'LL PULL THROUGH, RIGHT? OUR SEVEN YEARS' SENTENCE WILL BE OVER SOON!

JUST TELL YOURSELF THIS, JOHN: A NEW LIFE IS STARTING FOR YOU, AND IT CAN'T BE WORSE THAN THE OLD ONE.

AND HOW WILL YOU GET BACK FROM WHERE YOU'LL BE, FOOL?

YOU'RE OFFERING ME THE JOB BECAUSE NO ONE ELSE WANTS IT.

WRONG. I'M OFFERING IT BECAUSE I KNOW YOUR VIRTUES. YOU'RE LOYAL, EFFECTIVE, SERIOUS, INTELLIGENT, AND SENSITIVE.

YOU SPEAK PORTUGUESE, KNOW A GOOD PART OF THE ROUTE, AND CARE ABOUT THE HEALTH OF YOUR MEN.

GO AHEAD. I'M READY FOR ANYTHING.

ARTHUR, DON'T TAKE THIS AS A BLOW TO YOUR PRIDE!

AND ALSO, BECAUSE... HOW SHOULD I PUT IT?

I MERELY WISHED TO SAY THAT YOU WERE WITHOUT FAMILIAL TIES... ANOTHER POINT IN YOUR FAVOUR.

PRECISELY WHAT I SAID: I'M AN OBSCURE CAPTAIN, UNWORLDLY. SOME BELIEVE I'VE NO AMBITION, AND I HAVE NEITHER WIFE NOR CHILD. IN SHORT, THE PERFECT VICTIM!

WHAT IF I SAID IT WAS THE CHANCE OF A LIFETIME! IF I ASSURED YOU THAT BECAUSE OF THIS UNDERTAKING YOU'D GO DOWN IN HISTORY?

EVAN, THERE'S NOTHING GLORIOUS ABOUT HAULING PRISONERS TO THE OTHER END OF THE WORLD!

WRONG AGAIN!

YOU'RE A CAPTAIN NOW. YOU'D BECOME A GOVERNOR STRAIGHT AWAY, WITH PRACTICALLY FULL POWER IN A COLONY WHERE YOU'D BE EFFECTIVELY BEYOND LONDON'S CONTROL!

NAME ME ONE OTHER NAVAL OFFICER WHO'S EVER WIELDED SUCH POWER IN THE HISTORY OF ENGLAND?

AND WHEN YOU RETURNED, YOU'D BE NAMED ADMIRAL, OF COURSE.

THE BAUBLES ARE QUITE SEDUCTIVE, BUT THE REALITY'S ENTIRELY DIFFERENT.

165

ARTHUR PHILLIP WAS **48** IN OCTOBER **1786**, FACED WITH THE GREATEST CHALLENGE OF HIS CAREER, FEAR IN THE PIT OF HIS STOMACH.

BLACK CAESAR, **22**, PONDERED HIS FATE AND SAW NOTHING AWAITING HIM BUT PAIN.

JOHN HUDSON, *12*, SLEPT THE SLEEP OF INJUSTICE.

"BLOW, BLOW, THOU WINTER WIND, THOU ART NOT SO UNKIND AS MAN'S INGRATITUDE," WROTE SHAKESPEARE.

THE FUTURE SEEMED DARK INDEED.

WHAT FUTURE THERE WAS.

DECEMBER 1786.

THE SCOTS MAGAZINE

ANY NEWS AS CHRISTMAS NEARS?

WELL... I JUST FOUND OUT ABOUT AN ASTONISHING STORY.

YOU KNOW THOSE PRISONERS THEY'RE TRANSFERRING TO BOTANY BAY?

THE SCOTS MAGAZINE

BOTANY BAY? NO, WHERE'S THAT?

WHY, BOTANY BAY! IN THE PACIFIC, NEW SOUTH WALES! COOK DISCOVERED IT!

IN A FEW DAYS THEY'LL SET SAIL WITH SEVERAL HUNDRED PRISONERS TO FOUND A PENAL COLONY!

SO FAR AWAY? BUT THAT'S MADNESS! WILL THERE BE MANY WOMEN AND CHILDREN?

YOU HIT THE NAIL ON THE HEAD! LISTEN TO THIS...

"THE PRISONERS CONDEMNED TO EXILE IN BOTANY BAY WERE LED FROM THEIR CELLS TO BE TAKEN TO PLYMOUTH, WHERE THE FLEET COMMANDEERED FOR THE GREAT JOURNEY AWAITED."

"AMONG THEM WAS A WOMAN, SUSANNAH HOLMES, AND HER CHILD OF SIX MONTHS."

"WAS THAT CHILD BORN IN GAOL? DO THEY LET MALE AND FEMALE PRISONERS CONSORT LIKE THAT?"

"MY DEAR, I FEAR THE LIFE AND MORES OF ENGLISH GAOLS ARE LARGELY UNKNOWN TO US. BUT THAT'S NOT THE ISSUE. OUR STORY CONTINUES."

MR. SIMPSON! PLEASE! YOU'RE A GOOD GUARD, ALWAYS UNDERSTANDING WITH THE PRISONERS. YOU MUST HELP ME!

I'M NOT ALLOWED TO TALK TO YOU, HOLMES!

LISTEN TO ME! THIS CHILD NEEDS ITS FATHER! WE MUSTN'T BE SEPARATED!

HENRY HAS TO COME TO PLYMOUTH! I'M BEGGING YOU, HELP US!

I'D RATHER DIE THAN LET MY WIFE AND CHILD LEAVE ME!

HONEST, SIMPSON! I KNOW VERY WELL WHY I'M HERE.

BUT I ALSO KNOW WHAT I'LL DO IF I'M NOT ALLOWED TO JOIN THEM!

QUIET, KABLE! YOU'RE JUST LIKE THE REST: FOUND A WOMAN IN GAOL AND TOOK ADVANTAGE.

WHAT HAVE YOU GOT TO DO WITH HER AND HER BABY? SINCE WHEN HAVE YOU HA ANY FATHERLY INSTINCT? JUST BE HAPP YOU'LL NEVER SEE THEM AGAIN.

ONLY SOMEONE WITHOUT A CHILD COULD SAY SUCH THINGS! YOU DON'T UNDERSTAND!

AYE, BEFORE IT WAS TRUE I DIDN'T CARE ABOUT TOTS! BUT I LOVE SUSANNAH, AND THAT BABY'S MY LIFE!

YOU'VE GOT NO RIGHT TO SPLIT UP FAMILIES LIKE THIS! THERE MUST BE SOME WAY WE CAN BE TOGETHER!

173

AFTER FRANÇOIS BOURGEON.

175

179

YOU THINK YOU CAN WALK IN AND SEE HIS EXCELLENCY JUST LIKE THAT? BY SHOWING UP AT THE HOME OFFICE?

LOOK, I KNOW LORD SYDNEY MUST BE A VERY BUSY AND EVEN INACCESSIBLE MAN, BUT I BELIEVE IT'S A MATTER OF THE HIGHEST IMPORTANCE.

PLEASE TELL HIM IT'S ABOUT THE FAMOUS PENAL COLONY IN BOTANY BAY THEY'RE LEAVING FOR IN A FEW DAYS.

I'LL WAIT AS LONG AS IT TAKES!

JUST OUR LUCK, MY DEAR SMITH.

YES, YOUR EXCELLENCY! I'LL NOTIFY MR. PITT'S OFFICE RIGHT AWAY.

I'M COUNTING ON YOU. I'M EXPECTED AT MY RESIDENCE IN KENT TONIGHT.

OF COURSE, YOUR EXCELLENCY!

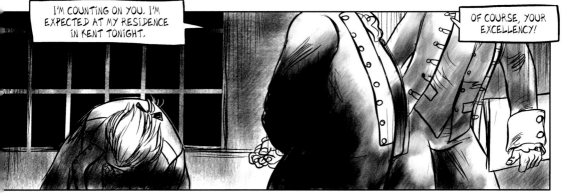

HUH?

I WONDER IF I WON'T LEAVE RIGHT NOW. I MUST SEE TO MY HORSES.

LORD SYDNEY!

WHAT'S THIS? WHO ARE YOU, SIR?

FORGIVE ME, YOUR EXCELLENCY! I'VE COME FROM NORWICH BY WAY OF PLYMOUTH, A GUARD FOR THE PRISONERS LEAVING FOR BOTANY BAY, BUT I SIMPLY MUST SEE YOU!

WO PRISONERS MEANT FOR TRANSPORTATION HAD A CHILD TOGETHER AT NORWICH.

THE WOMAN WAS JUST TRANSFERRED TO PLYMOUTH, BUT THE SHIP'S CAPTAIN WON'T HAVE HER CHILD ON BOARD.

I PROMISED TO PLEAD WITH YOU NOT TO BREAK THE SACRED TIES OF FAMILY WHICH, I ASSURE YOU, ARE PRESENT IN THIS CASE!

HOW QUICKLY YOU SPEAK, SIR!

PLEASE DON'T BE OFFENDED, YOUR EXCELLENCY. BUT SUMMING UP A SITUATION LIKE THIS ISN'T EASY.

I CAN TESTIFY THAT THIS FAMILY DOESN'T DESERVE TO BE TORN APART LIKE THIS.

YOU ARE BOLD, SIR! AND HAVE A CHARITABLE SOUL!

I AM AN OFFICER OF JUSTICE, AND SO AM CONCERNED WITH INJUSTICES.

COME WITH ME. I'LL GIVE YOU A FEW EXTRA MINUTES TO CONVINCE ME.

THANK YOU, YOUR EXCELLENCY.

CH KLI KLAK

KABLE! ON YOUR FEET!

GO TO HELL! LET ME DIE IN PEACE!

IN YOUR PLACE, I WOULDN'T GIVE UP SO EASY.

WHAT'S THIS BALDERDASH? I'VE NOTHING TO DO WITH THIS SCRAP OF PAPER!

THIS SCRAP OF PAPER, AS YOU CALL IT, BEARS THE SEAL OF LORD SYDNEY OF THE HOME OFFICE.

AND THEREFORE ACTING MINISTER OF WILLIAM PITT'S GOVERNMENT.

UNDER THE AUTHORITY OF HIS MAJESTY KING GEORGE, IN CASE YOU'RE UNAWARE.

QUIT YOUR MALARKEY. THERE'S NO AUTHORITY HERE BUT MINE.

XCEPT THAT IN THIS CASE — MEAN, THE DEPARTURE FOR BOTANY BAY — THE HOME CRETARY WILL OF COURSE BE EEPING AN EYE ON THINGS.

IN OTHER WORDS, DON'T LAY A HAND ON HENRY KABLE AND SUSANNAH HOLMES! OR THEIR CHILD.

I'LL TELL YOU WHAT YOU ARE, SIMPSON! AN IDEALIST! A STINKING IDEALIST!

AND YOU KNOW WHAT? YOU'RE MIXING UP PRISONERS AND GUARDS.

185

YOUR EXCELLENCY MAY BE AWARE THAT THE MATTER HE SETTLED IN FAVOUR OF THE "COUPLE" KABLE AND HOLMES WAS DIVULGED TO THE PUBLIC BY THE *SCOTS MAGAZINE*?

NO, I DIDN'T. BUT WE ARE QUITE PLEASED! IN ANY CASE, WE CHARGED MR. SMITH WITH ALERTING THE PRESS.

YES, AND OUR CONNECTIONS WORKED WELL, SINCE THE STORY WILL SOON ALSO BE TAKEN UP BY THE *GENTLEMAN'S MAGAZINE* AND *THE LONDON CHRONICLE*.

IT SEEMS THAT EVEN MISS BURNEY WISHES TO INCLUDE IT IN HER NEXT WORK.

CLEARLY THE PUBLIC LIKES A SENTIMENTAL STORY. MISS BURNEY, YOU SAY? DON'T KNOW HER.

WHAT A FARCE! NOTHING'S READY!

ARTHUR, CALM DOWN!

NO! I WILL NOT!

YOU KNOW AS WELL AS I DO THAT I'VE SENT THE ADMIRALTY DOZENS OF LETTERS, URGENT ONES FOR LORD SYDNEY.

THEY'VE ALL GONE UNANSWERED! IT'S AN INSULT!

WE HAVEN'T EVEN AN OFFICIAL LIST OF THE PRISONERS! HOW CAN WE HOPE TO FOUND A COLONY IN SUCH CONDITIONS?

THEY'RE CLEARLY NOT INTERESTED IN US.

WE NO LONGER COUNT IN THEIR EYES. IT'S AS IF WE'D ALREADY LEFT.

192

DO YOU EVEN REALIZE?

HOW WILL WE ENSURE OUR SUBSISTENCE ONCE WE'RE THERE, IF NO ONE CAN FISH OR FARM?

SURVIVAL INSTINCT? PROVIDENCE, PERHAPS?

IS GOVERNOR PHILLIP HERE? I'M FROM THE SECRETARY.

HE'S DOWN BELOW WITH HIS AIDE-DE-CAMP, PHILIP GIDLEY KING, SIR.

LOOK AT THIS POOR WOMAN. NO SHOES OR WARM CLOTHES. IT'S MARCH AND SHE'S SHIVERING.

IN A FEW MONTHS, SHE'LL HAVE DROPPED DEAD FROM EXHAUSTION!

GOVERNOR PHILLIP?

I AM HE. WHAT'S THIS?

JAMES SMITH, SIR. FROM THE HOME OFFICE.

I HAVE VERY IMPORTANT OFFICIAL PAPERS FOR YOU.

ABOUT TIME! THIS WAY TO MY CABIN, MR. SMITH. WE'LL BE MORE COMFORTABLE THERE.

SURE WILL...

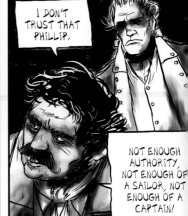

I DON'T TRUST THAT PHILLIP.

NOT ENOUGH AUTHORITY, NOT ENOUGH OF A SAILOR, NOT ENOUGH OF A CAPTAIN!

HE ROSE THROUGH THE RANKS, HE'S NO NOBLEMAN. HE WON'T BE SO HIGH-HANDED.

EVER HEARD OF SCURVY, LIEUTENANT CLARK?

VAGUELY, MR. WHITE. BUT AS CHIEF SURGEON I'M SURE YOU'LL TELL ME ALL ABOUT IT.

IT'S OUR GREATEST THREAT.

WHEN YOUR ARMS AND LEGS SWELL, AND YOUR NOSE AND GUMS BLEED, AND YOU DIE IN JUST A FEW HOURS!

MOST LONG VOYAGES AT SEA MEET WITH THAT FATE.

YOU'RE EXAGGERATING.

I AM NOT. YOU'D BE BETTER OFF WRITING TO YOUR WIF AND PREPARING FOR THE WORST.

196

HAVE A BIT OF THIS DELICIOUS PORT?

EVER SINCE SERVING IN THE PORTUGUESE NAVY, I'VE HAD A WEAKNESS FOR IT.

I KNOW YOU LIKE IT QUITE A BIT TOO, HUNTER!

INDEED, SIR.

...ER INTRODUCED ... BUT YOU KNOW ...AIN JOHN HUNTER, ...OF COURSE.

HE COMMANDS THE *SIRIUS* AND WILL REPLACE ME AS GOVERNOR SHOULD ANYTHING HAPPEN.

AN HONOUR, CAPTAIN HUNTER...

SO THESE ARE MY OFFICIAL ORDERS.

"IN THE KING'S NAME" OF COURSE...

"AND WHEREAS WE HAVE ORDERED THAT ABOUT 600 MALE, AND 180 FEMALE CONVICTS NOW UNDER SENTENCE OR ORDER OF TRANSPORTATION..."

YES, YES, GET ON WITH IT...

"IT IS OUR ROYAL WILL AND PLEASURE THAT YOU PROCEED TO THE PORT ON THE COAST OF NEW SOUTH WALES, SITUATED IN THE LATITUDE OF 33° 41' CALLED BY THE NAME OF BOTANY BAY."

"IT IS THEREFORE OUR WILL AND PLEASURE THAT YOU DO IMMEDIATELY UPON YOUR LANDING, AFTER TAKING MEASURES FOR SECURING YOURSELF AND THE PEOPLE WHO ACCOMPANY YOU, AS MUCH AS POSSIBLE, FROM ANY ATTACKS OR INTERRUPTIONS OF THE NATIVES OF THAT COUNTRY..."

"PROCEED TO THE CULTIVATION OF THE LAND, DISTRIBUTING THE CONVICTS FOR THAT PURPOSE IN SUCH MANNER AS MAY APPEAR TO YOU TO BE NECESSARY FOR PROCURING SUPPLIES OF GRAIN AND GROUND PROVISIONS."

"YOU ARE TO ENDEAVOUR BY EVERY POSSIBLE MEANS TO OPEN AN INTERCOURSE WITH THE NATIVES AND TO CONCILIATE THEIR AFFECTIONS, ENJOINING ALL OUR SUBJECTS TO LIVE IN AMITY AND KINDNESS WITH THEM."

"YOU SHALL HAVE FULL POWER TO UPHOLD THE RITES OF THE CHURCH OF ENGLAND, TO APPOINT JUDGES..."

"TO DECLARE IF NEED BE MARTIAL LAW, TO DISTRIBUTE TITLES AND PROPERTY, TO ORGANIZE BARTERS, AND REGULATE THE MARKETS THAT WILL NECESSARILY BE IMPLEMENTED."

"IT IS FURTHER OUR ROYAL WILL AND PLEASURE THAT YOU SURVEY THE COASTS AND TAKE THE NECESSARY MEASURES TO DEFEND THIS TERRITORY BY WHICH WE, GEORGE III, INTEND TO STRENGTHEN OUR EMPIRE."

SO THAT'S IT. FOUNDING A COLONY ISN'T ENOUGH.

I MUST ALSO FOUND AND ADMINISTER A NEW TERRITORY FOR THE CROWN!

IMPERIALISM ABOVE ALL!

YOU KNOW, ARTHUR....

IT WAS INCONCEIVABLE FOR SUCH A MISSION TO HAVE NO POLITICAL ELEMENT.

REMEMBER, THE FRENCH — THEIR FAMOUS LA PÉROUSE — ARE LIKELY LURKING NEARBY.

LA PÉROUSE ISN'T DANGEROUS.

HIS CIRCUMNAVIGATION IS ABOVE ALL IN THE NAME OF SCIENCE.

AND BESIDES, HE LEFT WHEN? TWO YEARS AGO? HE'LL BE EXHAUSTED IF HE EVEN REACHES BOTANY BAY.

NO, WHAT WORRIES ME IS THAT I HAVEN'T THE MEANS FOR THE KING'S AMBITION.

IN COMPARISON TO THESE NEW LANDS, IT'S AS IF HE'S ORDERED A COLONY OF ANTS TO CLIMB THE ALPS!

I WAS PICKED BY DEFAULT, BECAUSE I FOLLOW ORDERS WELL AND MAKE NO WAVES.

A PAWN EASILY MOVED FAR FROM HOME, EASILY SACRIFICED SHOULD THINGS GO WRONG.

IN ANY CASE, I RESIGNED FROM MY POST AT THE HOME OFFICE YESTERDAY.

I'M LEAVING WITH YOU.

HOW'S THAT?

AS AN OBSERVER?

NO, AS A FREE EMIGRANT.

I'M READY TO CHANGE MY LIFE, AND I'M CONVINCED THIS EXPEDITION AMOUNTS TO A HISTORIC MOMENT, PERHAPS ONE THAT WILL HERALD A NEW AGE OF MASS TRANSPORTATION!

I'VE CONSIDERED THIS AT LENGTH.

I SHALL ACCOMPANY YOU, AND I WANT TO HELP.

I DON'T KNOW IF YOU'RE THE MOST IDEALISTIC OR MERELY THE MADDEST MAN IN THIS COUNTRY, BUT...

YOUR WORDS HAVE TOUCHED MY HEART.

SO YOU ARE THE FIRST FREE COLONIST OF OUR FUTURE COLONY...

WELCOME ABOARD, MR. SMITH!

I WON'T SAY IT'LL BE EASY.

THANK YOU, CAPTAIN! I'LL HOLD YOU TO THAT!

YOU SURE TOOK YOUR SWEET TIME!

BACK TO SLEEP, JOHN HUDSON, YOU'RE TOO YOUNG YET.

FOR NOW.

205

ANOTHER PROBLEM WITH THE RUM?

NOT FOR US. THE HOME OFFICE CONFIRMED THAT THE SOLDIERS' ALCOHOL RATIONS WOULD BE RAISED, AND THEY KNOW IT.

THEIR DEMANDS ARE NOW GROUNDLESS. MAJOR ROSS HAS CONFIRMED IT.

OH, ROSS! HIS TROUBLEMAKING HAS ONLY JUST BEGUN, I GUARANTEE IT.

STILL, IT'S RATHER UNFORTUNA THAT THE HEAD OF OUR ARMY DETACHMENT IS SO UNPLEASAN

WHAT'S THE PROBLEM, THEN?

IT'S THE SAILORS THIS TIME. APPARENTLY THEY HAVEN'T BEEN PAID FOR SEVEN MONTHS.

THAT'S ALL WE NEEDED. THEY'RE CLEARLY IN THE RIGHT.

THERE CAN BE NO MORE DELAYS! WE'RE ALREADY SURE TO HIT STORM SEASON AFTER GOOD HOPE. WE MUST LEAVE IMMEDIATELY!

CAN'T DO ANYTHING WITHOUT THE SAILORS...

I KNOW. I'LL WRITE TO NEPEAN NOW AND ASK HIM AGAIN TO SETTLE THE MATTER RIGHT AWAY.

HE'LL SAY THE EXPEDITION'S ALREADY OVER BUDGET, BUT IT CAN'T BE HELPED.

ON THE OTHER HAND, I AM OBLIGED TO SHOW A FIRM HAND.

JOHN, REASSURE THE SAILORS, BUT FIND OUT WHO THE LEADERS OF THIS MOVEMENT ARE, AND I'LL HAVE THEM BOOTED OUT FROM THE CREW.

EXCHANGE THEM FOR SAILORS FROM OUR ESCORT, OR SOMETHING, BUT GET RID OF THEM!

SEA'S CALM, AIR'S WARM, A LIGHT SOUTHWESTERLY BREEZE. THE PRISONERS ARE ASLEEP, THE SAILORS HAVE BEEN PAID...

YOU THINKING WHAT I'M THINKING?

AYE... TONIGHT'S THE NIGHT!

"MY DEAR BELOVED WIFE BETSY, I WILL NEVER FORGIVE THE ADMIRALTY FOR NOT LETTING OFFICERS' WIVES ACCOMPANY THEIR HUSBANDS ON THIS VOYAGE..."

"NOR CAPTAIN PHILLIP FOR NOT GRANTING ANY LEAVE THESE LAST MONTHS."

"I HAVE BEGUN BITTERLY TO REGRET SWAPPING MY POSITION FOR A PASSAGE TO BOTANY BAY."

"I SHALL BE PROMOTED, OF COURSE, BUT AT WHAT PRICE?"

"THAT OF NOT SEEI YOU, OR OUR DEA LITTLE RALPH..."

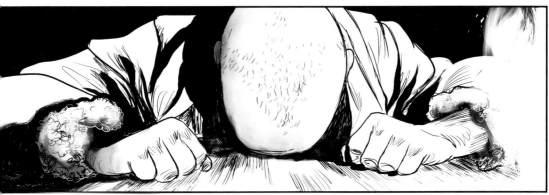

GOD, GIVE ME STRENGTH!

SUNDAY, 13 MAY 1787. THE FLEET LEAVES AT DAWN.

Book II
The Voyage

"*Onward to gold, marble, coralline lands,*
Ever by harsh lashing winds broadly fanned,
Their wakes intertwining from sea to sea,
Fleet as thoughts do the sailing ships speed."

Emile Verhaeren
(*Les Forces tumultueuses*, 1902)

BLEAARRGGH!

213

SEE WHAT A MESS IT IS, DOCTOR?

AND THAT SMELL! IT'S UNBEARABLE! THEY'RE ALL SICK!

TO BE EXPECTED.

HOW'S THAT?

THINK, LIEUTENANT

214

E STAYED ANCHORED IN PORTSMOUTH FOR WEEKS.

NOW THAT WE'RE MOVING, THEY'RE SEASICK!

ALREADY?

THAT'S RIGHT! I'D HAVE BEEN SURPRISED IF THEY WEREN'T.

BUT... WHAT DO WE DO?

NOTHING.

WE WAIT. IT'LL DIE DOWN.

IT'S A VERY LONG TRIP. THEY'LL GET USED TO IT.

BESIDES...

DIARY OF 2ND LIEUTENANT RALPH CLARK.

"MY DEAR BETSY, WE SET OUT FOUR DAYS AGO, AND TROUBLE STARTED UP RIGHT AWAY."

"THE PRISONERS ARE SICK AN VOMITING ALL THE TIME."

"YESTERDAY, ABOARD THE *CHARLOTTE,* A CORPORAL SOMEHOW SHOT HIMSELF IN THE FOOT WITH HIS OWN RIFLE."

"IN THE HOLD, WE SLAUGHTE SHEEP FOR FOOD. I AM ALL BUT SURE THAT RATIONING WILL SOON BE UPON US."

"IN SHORT, THE FATE OF THIS EXPEDITION WORRIES ME. HOW I WISH I WERE WITH YOU AND OUR CHILD!"

"I MISS YOU TERRIBLY, AND I PROMISE TO WRITE EVERY DAY."

"AT OUR FIRST PORT OF CALL, I WILL TRY TO FIND A SHIP TO BRING YOU MY LETTERS."

"MEANWHILE, I SEND YOU TENDER KISSES AND THIN OF YOU ALWAYS, MY LOVE"

221

CONSIDER THE SITUATION, WILL YOU?

OUR PRISONERS ARE LARGELY FILLED WITH STRONG FEELINGS OF INJUSTICE, AND FEW OF THEM SEE THIS TRANSPORTATION AS A PROMISE OF BETTER DAYS.

SO? THEY'RE SERVING TIME!

OF COURSE, I THINK THIS ATTEMPT AT MUTINY IS MOSTLY SYMBOLIC, AND REFLECTS THEIR STATE OF MIND.

SYMBOLIC? DID I HEAR RIGHT? YOU'RE JOKING!

I'VE ALREADY DECIDED TO TRANSFER GRIFFITHS TO THE *PRINCE OF WALES*, BUT I WANT TO REDUCE THE NUMBER OF LASHES. SAY, 25.

WHAT? YOU CAN'T DO THIS!

DO YOU REALIZE HE TORTURED ONE OF HI CELLMATES FOR REFUS TO TAKE PART IN HIS SCHEME?

HE'S A SAVAGE! A BRUTE! HE DESERVES TO DIE!

THAT WOULD MAKE A MARTYR OF HIM, MAJOR ROSS. INSTEAD OF QUIETING THE SITUATION, IT WOULD EXACERBATE IT.

A MARTYR, YOU SAY? I SAY AN EXAMPLE!

I DON'T THINK SO. AT ANY RATE, I'LL TAKE THE RISK.

AND I'LL EVEN ORDER ALL IRONS TO BE REMOVED FROM PRISONERS ON THAT SHIP.

WHAT'S MORE, I CHARGE LIEUTENANT SHORTLAND HERE WITH STARTING A COMPREHENSIVE CENSUS OF ALL PRISONERS.

I... I DON'T UNDERSTAND YOU!

SURNAME, GIVEN NAME, TRADE BEFORE PRISON, OR AT LEAST SKILLS, AMBITIONS IN THE FUTURE COLONY, ETC.

IT'S TIME TO TRY AND GET OURSELVES ORGANIZED IF WE WANT TO SUCCEED!

YES, SIR. YOU'RE THE GOVERNOR.

HE WON'T LAST MUCH LONGER.

THE FLEET WILL BE RECORDING ITS FIRST LOSS, LIEUTENANT.

IS THERE REALLY NOTHING TO BE DONE?

NO, FEVER'S TOO HIGH...

IT'S OVER.

PLEASE NOTE THE TIME OF DEATH. MONDAY, 21 MAY 1787, WILLIAM MEAD, SAILOR ABOARD THE SCARBOROUGH.

WELL, THEN, HAVE TO TOSS HIM OVERBOARD QUICK AS WE CAN, AND HOPE SCURVY WON'T REAR ITS HEAD THIS TRIP.

THAT'S MY WORST FEAR, ALL THE WAY TO THE END.

NOT TO MENTION STORMS, CAPSIZINGS...

LET ALONE DESPAIR...

230

THE SAVAGE ISLANDS...

WE'RE NOT FAR FROM TENERIFE NOW. OUR FIRST PORT OF CALL.

YOU'RE THE ONLY CIVILIAN VOLUNTEER ON BOARD, MR. SMITH. DON'T THINK JUST BECAUSE WE BEAR THE SAME LAST NAME THAT I'LL BE LENIENT TOWARDS YOU.

WHATEVER ARE YOU DOING IN THIS HELLHOLE?

FIRSTLY, WE'RE A LETTER APART, MR. SMYTH. THAT MIGHT MAKE ALL THE DIFFERENCE!

I CAN TELL YOU'RE A GOOD DOCTOR: PRACTICAL, WHO'S TO SAY I'M NOT A DREAMER!

A FORMER CIVIL SERVANT FOR THE HOME OFFICE, BUT ALSO AN IDEALIST?

HMM... LET'S SAY THAT IN A WORLD OF POLITICIANS — THAT IS, SHARKS — I WAS MORE OF A FREETHINKER. A DOLPHIN.

I SEE... EXCEPT YOU DIVED INTO A WORLD OF PRISONERS AND BUTCHERS...

THAT IS, VULTURES AND VILLAINS.

DON'T WORRY, I'LL MAKE MY WAY.

AND YOU?

WELL...

DR. SMYTH! COME QUICKLY! IT'S URGENT!

234

YOU SUMMONED ME, SIR?

YES, DOCTOR.

WE'LL BE IN TENERIFE TOMORROW, AND THE SANTA [C]RUZ AUTHORITIES ARE BOUND TO [ASK] ABOUT HEALTH CONDITIONS. [W]HAT ARE THE FIGURES?

EIGHT DEATHS SINCE WE SET SAIL, SEVEN ADULTS AND ONE CHILD.

TWO BIRTHS HAVE BEEN RECORDED.

[92] PEOPLE ARE CURRENTLY ILL [IN] OUR 11 SHIPS. 72 PRISONERS AND 9 SOLDIERS.

I WAS EXPECTING WORSE.

YOU SURE ABOUT YOUR FIGURES, DR. WHITE?

NINE SICK SOLDIERS AND NOT A SINGLE SAILOR?

E GODS,
'T'S HOT!

I CAN'T BEAR IT!

AND YOU, MR.
VALLANCE? AREN'T
YOU TEMPTED TO FIND
SOME SHADE, WITH
THE PRISONERS?

UH... NO, LIEUTENANT!
AS 3RD CAPTAIN, I REALLY
HAVEN'T TIME, YOU KNOW, TO—

OH, COME NOW!

IT'S JUST US MEN HERE. I'VE
SPOTTED YOUR LITTLE GAME.

SIR, I ASSURE
YOU THAT—

ALL CONTACT WITH
PRISONERS IS FORBIDDEN!
I WON'T REPEAT MYSELF!

I'M SAYING
IT FOR YOUR
SAKE, YOU
KNOW.

LISTEN UP, THE LOT OF YOU!

E'RE OFF TENERIFE RIGHT W, OUR FIRST PORT OF CALL.

THERE'LL BE TWO OTHERS THIS TRIP, RIO AND THE CAPE.

IT'LL TAKE A FEW DAYS TO RESUPPLY THE FLEET WITH FOOD AND WATER.

TENERIFE IS UNDER SPANISH RULE. WE'RE GUESTS IN A FOREIGN COUNTRY AND HAVE PERMISSION TO DROP ANCHOR IN THE PORT OF SANTA CRUZ.

I DON'T NEED TO REMIND YOU I WON'T TOLERATE ANY INCIDENTS DURING OUR STAY!

I'VE GOT AN ESCAPE PLAN! YOU WITH ME, CAESAR?

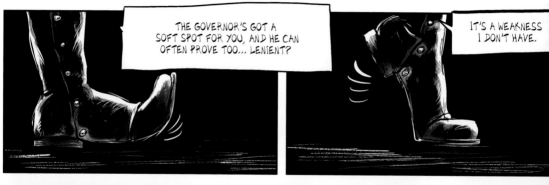

"WHAT'S THIS YOU'RE SAYING? A PRISONER'S ESCAPED FROM THE ALEXANDER?"

"HE SLIPPED OVER THE SIDE WHILE A SPANISH BOAT WAS RESTOCKING US. NO ONE SAW HIM AT THE TIME."

"GOOD GOD! WHEN WAS THIS?"

"THIS AFTERNOON, SIR. HIS NAME'S JOHN POWER."

"WE'RE GOING TO FIND THAT SON OF A BITCH. HE CAN'T BE FAR! THE SPANIARDS AREN'T HIDING HIM, ARE THEY?"

FIRST HE WAS ON THEIR [SHI]P, BUT THEN HE JUMPED AND SWAM OFF.

HE CAN'T HAVE GONE FAR. CAN'T IMAGINE HE'D GO TO SANTA CRUZ. HE'D BE SPOTTED IMMEDIATELY.

HE MUST'VE HEADED FOR OPEN WATER. THERE ARE ISLETS OUT THERE.

SEARCH THE SECTOR RIGHT AWAY!

241

HAVE A GOOD NIGHT, MR. POWER?

NOOOOOOO!

DAMN THIS HEAT! YOU COULD COOK AN EGG ON THIS DECK!

HOW LONG ARE YOU IN FOR?

SEVEN YEARS, YOU?

SAME.. WELL, NOT AT FIRST. THOSE BASTARDS SENTENCED ME TO DIE.

JUST FOR STEALING A FEW THINGS.

IMAGINE!

248

YOU MARRIED?

I GUESS SO...
I GOT MYSELF A WOMAN.
WE'VE A TYKE TOGETHER
ALREADY. THEY PUT US
ALL ON THIS BOAT.

CAN'T COMPLAIN.

YOU NEVER LAIN WITH
A WOMAN, I BET?

UH... NO.

YOU'LL GET THE HANG
OF IT RIGHT QUICK. IT'S
ONLY NATURAL!

BESIDES, IT'S
THE ONLY WAY TO KILL
TIME HERE. EVERYONE'S
TRYING TO FUCK!

THE ONES WHO
SAY THEY AREN'T
ARE LYING!

"MY DEAREST BETSY, THE HEAT IS STIFLING. STORMS OFTEN BREAK OUT, AND SOMETIMES THE LIGHTNING IS RED."

"TODAY IS OUR 3RD WEDDING ANNIVERSARY. I THINK OF YOU AND OUR BELOVED SON ALL THE TIME."

"TODAY WE LEFT THE WOMEN INSIDE, IN THE SHADE."

"MANY FAINTED ALL THE SAME, ALMOST SUFFOCATING."

"HOWEVER, I HAD TO PUNISH THOSE FIVE HARPIES AGAIN. THEY HAUNT ME DAY AND NIGHT."

"THEY'RE REAL WITCHES, DISGUSTING AND DEPRAVED!"

"WHY ARE THEY EVEN ON BOARD?"

"WE'LL BE OVER THE EQUATOR BEFORE LONG, WHICH PROVES THE FLEET IS ADVANCING SWIFTLY."

"GOD KNOWS WHAT HORIZONS THE NEW HEMISPHERE HAS IN STORE..."

SAILORS! SPECIAL PERMISSION TO SWIM!

HOORAY!

THANKS, CAPTAIN!

NOT A MINUTE TOO SOON!

LAST ONE IN'S BUYING RUM IN RIO!

ARE YOU SURE, CAPTAIN? IS THIS PRUDENT?

DON'T WORRY, LIEUTENANT. I KNOW WHAT MY MEN NEED, OR ELSE THEY'LL STOP WORKING!

SHIT! ALWAYS GETTING SPECIAL TREATMENT!

WELL... THEY'RE FREE.

DID YOU HEAR THAT?

THE SAILORS ARE SWIMMING!

WHILE WE'RE ROTTING AWAY...

252

WHERE'S MY SON?

IN HIS CABIN, SIR. I THINK HIS CONDUCT HAS BEEN SATISFACTORY.

HE'S ONLY EIGHT, BUT AT HIS AGE ONE BEGINS TO SEE THE REALITY OF THINGS...

THAT THE WORLD REQUIRES FORCE AND ORDER.

OR ELSE—CHAOS!

HE'LL BE A SOLDIER LIKE ME. MAY THIS MISSION GIVE HIM A REAL SENSE OF VALUES!

SPEAKING OF VALUES, I MUST SPEAK TO YOU ABOUT PRIVATES RYAN AND DOUGHERTY.

DON'T KNOW 'EM.

THEY'RE ON THE *PRINCE OF WALES*, UNDER ARREST FOR DISOBEDIENCE AND INSULTING THEIR SUPERIORS, AWAITING COURT MARTIAL.

HMPH! BAD SEEDS! I WAS A YOUNG SOLDIER IN THE SEVEN YEARS WAR, AND I NEVER DISOBEYED AN ORDER!

YOU THINK I EVER INSULTED MY COMMANDING OFFICERS IN THE WAR OF INDEPENDENCE?

NO, SIR, CERTAINLY NOT!

I CAN NO MORE TOLERATE [LI]P'S ANGELIC AND GUILTILY [I]NDULGENT WAYS TOWARDS [TH]E PRISONERS THAN I CAN THE [SL]IGHTEST INSUBORDINATION IN MY RANKS!

ARRANGE FOR A COURT MARTIAL. PREPARE THEIR TRANSFER!

BUT.... NOW?

ABSOLUTELY! BRING THEM ABOARD THE *SIRIUS* AS SOON AS POSSIBLE! I WON'T LET THIS AFFAIR DRAG ON!

YES, SIR. I JUST HOPE THAT WITH THE STORM COMING ON—

THAT'LL GIVE THEM A SENSE OF THE VALUES WE WERE JUST DISCUSSING.

DISMISSED!

258

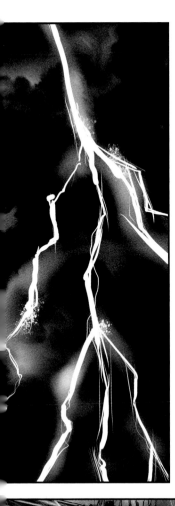

RYAN, YOUR INSOLENCE IS UNACCEPTABLE AND WILL BE PUNISHED.

DOUGHERTY, YOU'RE HERE FOR DISOBEDIENCE AND THAT'S EQUALLY INTOLERABLE.

WE WERE EXPECTING TO HEAR THAT YOUR WIFE WAS PREGNANT.

UH... YES, SIR, EIGHT MONTHS, SIR. SHE'LL GIVE BIRTH SOON.

IN THAT CASE, NO POINT TELLING YOU YOU'RE AN UTTER IDIOT! SHOULDN'T YOU BE A MODEL HUSBAND AND IMPECCABLE SOLDIER?

THIS TIME, GIVEN THE CIRCUMSTANCES, THE COURT PARDONS YOU.

AS FOR YOU, RYAN...

300 LASHES OF THE WHIP.

263

MONDAY, 6 AUGUST
1787.
ARRIVAL IN RIO.

267

OH, IT'S YOU, SIR! FORGIVE ME, I DIDN'T HEAR YOU COMING.

AT EASE, LIEUTENANT.

YOUR NAME?

WILLIAM DAWES, 2ND LIEUTENANT ABOARD THE SIRIUS!

YES, I REMEMBER YOUR FILE. AN ASTRONOMER, AREN'T YOU?

I'VE SOME LITTLE SKILL...

...ET'S HOPE YOU'LL HAVE MORE ...CK THAN COOK WITH HIS TRANSIT ... VENUS! WHEN I THINK ABOUT IT! WHAT A FIASCO!

AH, ASTRONOMY... A SCIENCE BASED ON THE EXACT POSITION OF CELESTIAL BODIES AND THEIR OH SO PREDICTABLE MOVEMENTS...

YES... UH CERTAINLY.

YOU'RE RIGHT TO! WHAT AN ANALOGY FOR AN ASTRONOMER! GOD IS THE STAR THAT BURNS BRIGHTEST IN THE NIGHT AND GUIDES US!

OF COURSE....

"BUT THE PATH TO HIM... OR TO THAT LIGHT! MEN MUST TRAVEL IT..."

AND THEREIN LIES THE WHOLE PROBLEM.

YES.

HAPPY WATCHING, MR. DAWES.

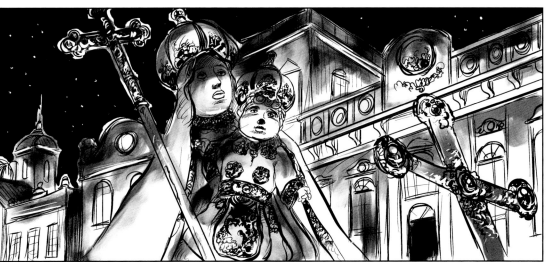

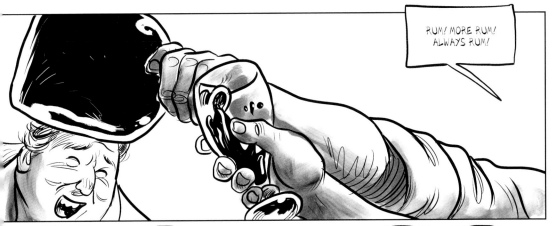

RUM! MORE RUM! ALWAYS RUM!

"NO MATTER WHAT THEY SAY, IT'S TRUE I WAS A LONELY BOY, NO STRENGTH, NO DREAMS..."

TO YOUR HEALTH, FRIENDS! KEEP SINGING WITHOUT ME, I'LL BRING THE RAIN IF I KEEP GOING!

"BUT IN THE WAKE OF THINGS, IT'S A FUNNY CRIME..."

OOPS! I DON'T FEEL WELL....

COMING THROUGH! NAUSEA EMERGENCY!

"THE BIRD'S UP IN THE AIR, BUT ITS EYES CAN'T SEE WHAT'S LEFT..."

BLEUURGGH!

278

IT'S A SONG... A KIND OF CHANTING... ALMOST A LAMENT.

"SO MERMAIDS DO EXIST?"

"THANKFULLY NOT, OR WE'D BE LOST! IT'S NOT FROM THE WATER, BUT THAT BOAT."

I KNOW WHAT IT IS.

THAT'S A SLAVER BEFORE YOU, GENTS.

ND WHAT YOU'RE HEARING..."

"ARE THE INCANTATIONS OF SLAVES! HAPPENS ALMOST EVERY NIGHT. BUT IT'S RARE TO HEAR IT SO CLEARLY."

"CAN'T HEAR THEM ANY MORE."

"AYE, THEY'VE STOPPED."

MOVING AND CAPTIVATING...

CHILLING, YOU MEAN!

PICK UP WHERE WE LEFT OFF?

AFTER A SAD SHOW LIKE THAT? WHY PILE MISFORTU ON MISFORTUNE?

PARTY'S RUINED...

I'M GOING TO LIE DOWN.

AND ME FOR A WALK ON DECK.

MY FRIENDS, MAY THAT SLAVE SONG NOT HAUNT US FOR THE REST OF OUR LIVES...

CLAC

UP, MR. DAWES! AND LET ME HEAR THE SOUND OF YOUR VOICE, PLEASE.

FORGIVE ME, SIR. I WAS FAS ASLEEP. UP LATE... SORR

DID YOU HEAR THE SLAVES SINGING LAST NIGHT?

I THOUGHT IT WAS TIME TO LEAVE. HOW LONG HAVE WE BEEN IN RIO?

EXACTLY 29 DAYS.

THE GOVERNOR SAW FIT TO KEEP US HERE OVER SOME UNPAID BILL...

AS IF OUR RESUPPLY WERE REMOTELY SATISFACTORY!

ALL PART OF THE GAME, I SUPPOSE.

I DON'T KNOW IF WE'RE REALLY READY TO HOLD OUT PAST THE CAPE. WE'LL HAVE TO REVIEW OUR RATIONING PLAN.

WE'LL NEED MORE THAN A MONTH TO GET THERE.

HAVE NEWS FROM LONDON. THEY'RE READYING PACIFIC EXPEDITION TO SEARCH FOR BREADFRUIT.

THE CAPTAIN'S ONE OF COOK'S OLD BOATSWAINS WHO WAS MADE LIEUTENANT: ONE WILLIAM BLIGH.

I ONLY KNOW HIM BY NAME. WHAT SHIP IS IT?

AN OLD COLLIER CALLED THE *BETHIA.* THEY'VE RENOVATED IT AND CHRISTENED IT THE *BOUNTY.* IF ALL GOES WELL, THEY'LL BE IN BOTANY BAY NEXT YEAR. I HOPE THEY CAN RESUPPLY US.

YOU DO PLAN AHEAD, ARTHUR.

CHRIST! WE'RE ALL GOING OVER!

HOLD FAST, JOHN! THIS CAN'T LAST ALL DAY!

HERE, YOU TRY!

WE'RE IN SERIOUS DANGER. THE LOWER DECK MIGHT FLOOD AT ANY MOMENT!

WE ALL JUST DECIDED TO FORGO OUR RUM RATION FOR TODAY! THE WORK'S TOO HARD AND TOO IMPORTANT! YOU WITH US?

AYE, I'M WITH YOU! SAILOR'S WORD! WHEN THE GOING GETS TOUGH, WE'RE THERE FOR EACH OTHER!

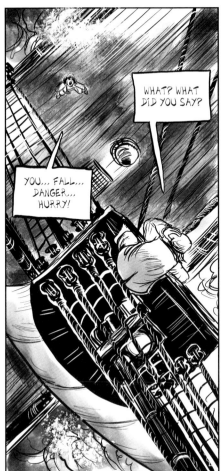

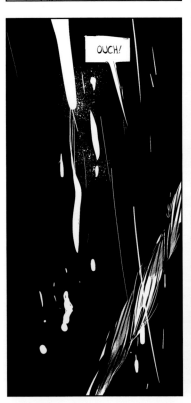
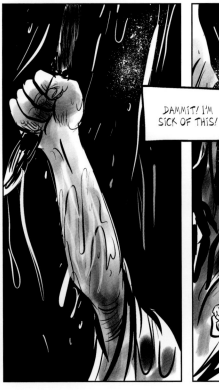

URRGGGGHHHH!!!!

CALM DOWN NOW AND PUSH HARDER! BOTH YOUR LIVES DEPEND ON IT!

THIS HAD TO HAPPEN DURING THE STORM, DIDN'T IT?

AAAHHHHHH!!!!

ENOUGH! THIS WON'T DO! WHAT'S YOUR NAME, GIRL?

HEY! STOP THAT!

YOUR NAME!

MARY... MARY BROAD.

YOU'RE GOING TO FIGHT FOR YOUR CHILD, MARY. BY GOD I SWEAR IT!

THERE! SHE'S SHOWING! KEEP GOING, MARY!

THERE! A LITTLE GIRL!

SOMEDAY YOUR MOTHER'LL HAVE TO TELL YOU HOW YOU CAME INTO THE WORLD!

THIS STORM WAS NOTHING COMPARED TO YOU!

MY BABY... MY LITTLE GIRL... YOU'RE STRONG. THAT'S GOOD.

YOU'RE BOTH STRONG!

HER NAME?

YOU WERE BORN ON THIS SHIP... THE CHARLOTTE.

SO I'LL CALL HER CHARLOTTE!

DR. WHITE! BACK WITH US TODAY, ARE YOU?

HELLO, CLARK. DOING MY ROUNDS, ACTUALLY.

I WAS ON THE *CHARLOTTE* LAST WEEK. I'M ON THE *FRIENDSHIP* TILL TOMORROW, THEN THE *SCARBOROUGH* AFTER THAT.

HOW'S THE FLEET?

THE GOVERNOR'S NOT VERY HAPPY. HE THINKS THE SHIPS SHOULD BE CLOSER TOGETHER.

WHAT? DID YOU SEE THOSE STORMS? IT'S ALREADY A MIRACLE WE'RE ALL STILL ALIVE AND THERE WEREN'T ANY WRECKS!

YOU'RE TELLING ME. BUT HE INTENDS TO REMOBILIZE OUR FORCES. HE THINKS WE'RE DRIFTING APART.

NOW THAT TAKES THE BISCUIT! SOMETIMES I JUST DON'T UNDERSTAND HIM.

HAVE YOU SEEN THE "HARPIES", AS I CALL THEM?

YES, YOUR FIVE USUALLY IN LOCKUP, INCLUDING FOUR ELIZABETHS! WOMEN OF SPIRIT...

YOU SHOULD KNOW THAT PULLY AND MCCORMICK ARE PREGNANT.

IT CAN'T BE! THAT DISGUSTS ME. I CAN'T STAND THOSE...

THOSE ANIMALS! BEASTS! STRUMPETS!

CALL IT WHAT YOU WILL — NATURE, INSTINCTS, BASIC NEEDS — LIFE ALWAYS FINDS A WAY AND WINS OUT.

YOU'RE VERY UNDERSTANDING. WHAT DO YOU THINK THOSE CHILDREN'S LIVES WILL BE LIKE?

BORN IN POVERTY TO HUSBANDLESS WOMEN SENTENCED TO TRANSPORTATION AND SOON TO BE ON THE OTHER SIDE OF THE WORLD WITHOUT RESOURCES?

I ADMIRE YOUR COLD LOGIC, LIEUTENANT, BUT I'M NOT SURE IT'S THE RIGHT ATTITUDE.

WE'RE HEADED STRAIGHT FOR THE UNKNOWN, AND EVERY PASSING SECOND BRINGS US MORE HOPE AND LIFE. NOTHING RATIONAL ABOUT IT! NOTHING WRITTEN, NOTHING ORDAINED. ALL IS YET TO BE DISCOVERED!

YOU SEE ADVENTURE. I SEE A MISSION.

YOU'LL CHANGE YOUR MIND, CLARK. YOU'LL CHANGE YOUR MIND.

SATURDAY 13 OCTOBER 1787. ARRIVAL AT THE CAPE.

306

HE WAS SHOUTING THAT HE ULDN'T STAND BEING APART FROM SOME PRISONER ANY MORE.

ONE OF THE WOMEN YOU HAD TRANSFERRED TO THE *PRINCE OF WALES* A FEW DAYS AGO.

VERITABLE HARPIES, THOSE WOMEN! NO ONE COULD STAND THEM!

EXCEPT MR. VALLANCE, APPARENTLY. HE SAID HE LOVED HER AND WANTED TO MARRY HER. HE MUST'VE GOT TOO CLOSE TO THE EDGE AND A SWELL WAS ENOUGH TO...

GOOD GOD... ALL FOR THAT!

SORRY, SIR. NO TRACE OF A BODY!

SAY, COULD WE GET BACK ON? OR ELSE WE MIGHT DIE TOO... WATER'S FREEZING!

HOLD ON TIGHT, MAJOR!

THIS DECK IS POORLY MAINTAINED.

WHERE IS HE?

I'M LIEUTENANT KELLOW. THIS WAY, SIR. HE'S WAITING.

RiiiGHT...
SO WHERE'S HE
FROM?

F I UNDERSTAND
ORRECTLY, HE'S A
ENTRY FROM ONE
F THE GARRISONS
IN TOWN.

HE MADE A GREAT EFFORT
TO SWIM OUT. HE WANTS
TO STAY WITH US!

PLEASE... I SPEAKING
ENGLISH BAD... I WANT
HERE STAY.

NOT HAPPY ON
CAPE. I... UNHAPPY!
BOAT, HOPE!

I SOLDIER.
I SERVING
ENGLAND!

313

HE MIGHT HOLD OUT FOR THE TRIP, BUT ONCE WE GET TO BOTANY BAY, THAT'S A DIFFERENT STORY.

IF WE GET THERE!

DID YOU SEE THE DANISH SHIP THAT JUST ARRIVED THE OTHER DAY?

PRACTICALLY A WRECK! ALMOST DESTROYED BY STORMS!

PLUS I HEARD ITS CAPTAIN DIED IN THE CHAOS!

WHAT WORRIES ME IS THE ORDER OF THE FLEET IN BAD WEATHER.

WE'LL NEVER BE ABLE TO STAY TOGETHER IN THE INDIAN OCEAN!

YES, THE HARDEST PART IS SURELY YET TO COME.

THE GOVERNOR'LL NEVER RISK SPLITTING THE FLEET UP!

STILL, IT MIGHT BE A GOOD IDEA IF AT LEAST ONE BOAT ARRIVES BEFORE THE OTHERS AND PREPARES THE GROUND A BIT.

NO ONE WILL PREPARE ANYTHING! WE NEED EVERYONE'S HELP TO SET UP SUCH A LARGE COLONY, AND—

AAAAAH!

WHO... WHO ARE YOU? YOU SPEAK ENGLISH?

I SPEAK MANY TONGUES! ESPECIALLY THAT OF OUR WORLD'S BUTCHERS!

EXCUSE ME! WE ARE NOT SLAVERS!

NO, BUT YOU SHIP YOUR PRISONERS LIKE CATTLE.

THEY'RE GOING TO START A NEW COUNTRY! BETTER THAN ROTTING IN A CELL!

THE MAN YOU SEE THERE CAME TO YOU A FREE MAN. AND YOU REFUSED HIM WHAT YOU GRANT YOUR CONVICTS?

WE CAN'T TAKE ON ALL THE WORLD'S RE—

DO YOU KNOW WHAT THEY DID TO HIM WHEN YOU BROUGHT HIM BACK?

THEY BROKE HIS BONES ONE BY ONE! FIRST HIS ARMS, THEN HIS LEGS...

SHARP, SWIFT HAMMER BLOWS, TO MAKE HIM SCREAM.

THEN THEY HANGED HIM, BUT HE WAS STILL ALIVE THEN.

HE ENDURED HIS TORTURE RIGHT UP TO THE END, BECAUSE HE'S DARED DREAM OF A FUTU A NEW LIFE...

SHE'S NAMED THE *FRIENDSHIP!* LIKE US.

SHE'S FROM THE AMERICAS.

LOOKS LIKE WE'RE NOT LEAVING TODAY.

THAT SHIP'S IN OUR WAY!

IF YOU SAY SO, SIR.

THEY'RE HEADED STRAIGHT FOR THE *SIRIUS!*

"I KNEW THE GOVERNO WOULD BE INTERESTE IN THEM."

THANK YOU FOR COMING, CAPTAIN.

NOT AT ALL, SIR. MAY I SAY IT STILL FEELS STRANGE, BEING AMONG ENGLISHMEN.

BUT WE'RE TWO INDEPENDENT NATIONS, AND SO CAN SPEAK DIPLOMATICALLY.

WHERE ARE YOU FROM?

BOSTON.

WHAT'S THE SITUATION THERE?

WE'RE GETTING ALONG AS BEST WE CAN. PEACE IS BACK AND BUSINESS GROWING EVERY YEAR, AS MY PRESENCE HERE ATTESTS.

ARMY AS DISORGANIZED AS EVER, I TAKE IT?

W SEE, WON OUR EEDOM.

MAJOR ROSS! CAN'T YOU BE POLITE JUST THIS ONCE!

THE DIFFERENCE BETWEEN MEN WITH VISION AND MEN WITH GUNS!

319

EVER HEARD OF A FRENCHMAN NAMED LA PÉROUSE? KNOW WHERE HE IS NOW?

NO, SORRY, CAN'T SAY I DO. WHERE ARE YOU AND YOUR FLEET HEADED?

BOTANY BAY, IN THE SOUTH PACIFIC, TO FOUND A COLONY.

THAT'S ABOUT WHAT I HEARD. YOU CALL THAT SPOT NEW SOUTH WALES, RIGHT?

EXACTLY.

VIRGIN TERRITORY, APT TO STIR DREAMS AND ASPIRATIONS.

BELIEVE ME, IT COULD SOON BE A PLACE THAT DRAWS EMIGRANTS.

OR NIGHTMARES!

WE AMERICANS, FOR ONE, HAVE ADVENTUROUS SPIRITS AND A THIRST FOR NOVELTY.

MONDAY, 12
NOVEMBER 1787.
LEAVING THE CAPE.

"MY DEAREST BETSY, WE LEFT THE CAPE
AFTER A MONTH OR SO. STRANGELY ENOUGH,
NO PRISONER WAS SHOUTING OR EVEN SPOKE."

"EVERYONE ON DECK WAS
SOMBRE AS WELL."

"AND TELLING YOURSELF THAT WE'D EITHER PERISH AT SEA, OR DISCOVER A NEW LAND! EITHER CASE WOULD MAKE THE HISTORY BOOKS."

"ALL OUR CALCULATIONS SHOW IT WILL TAKE AROUND NINE MONTHS TO REACH THE END OF OUR JOURNEY."

"SO I SUPPOSE WE'VE A RIGHT TO BE PROUD..."

"OF HAVING BROUGHT A NEW WORLD INTO BEING."

"A FLOWER THE SIZE OF A CONTINENT AWAITS US, AND WE'RE TO BE ITS POLLEN."

IF ALL GOES WELL, WE SHOULD REACH OUR DESTINATION IN A MONTH.

WHICH COMES TO... ABOUT 250 DAYS AT SEA? NO SHAME IN THAT!

INDEED. STILL, I WORRY ABOUT HAVING SPLIT THE FLEET IN TWO.

WITH THESE DIFFICULT WEATHER CONDITIONS, ELEVEN SHIPS WOULD NEVER'VE STAYED TOGETHER ALL THE WAY TO BOTANY BAY! THE LAGGARDS WOULD SLOW THE FASTEST TOO MUCH.

OF COURSE, MR. COLLINS. THAT'S WHAT I TOLD MYSELF BUT WHAT IF I WAS WRONG? FOUR SHIPS UP FRONT, SEVEN BEHIND, GOD KNOWS WHERE... WHAT IF THEY RUN INTO TROUBLE?

YOU'VE ENTRUSTED THEM TO MR. HUNTER. NOTHING TO FEAR!

AND WE'LL PREPARE THE GROUND FOR THE REST TO ARRIVE, RIGHT?

STOP TORMENTING YOURSELF, ARTHUR! YOU'VE MADE YOUR DECISION. ANYWAY, THE DIE IS CAST.

LAND HO!

WE SIGHTED VAN DIEMEN'S LAND ON 3 JANUARY 1788. MAKE A NOTE.

GRAB YOUR SPYGLASS, PHILIP....

WHAT AM I LOOKING FOR?

NATIVES.

"I SEE SMOKE RISING FROM THE TREES. NO DOUBT A NATIVE ENCAMPMENT."

"THEY SPOTTED US RIGHT AWAY! IT'S A SIGN AND A SYMBOL. THIS IS THEIR HOME, AFTER ALL."

"IN TRUTH, I DREAD OUR FIRST CONFRONTATION."

NOW ALL WE HAVE TO DO IS SAIL NORTH UP THE COAST.

JUST A MATTER OF DAYS!

AND WE'LL FINALLY BE ABLE TO PUT AN END TO THIS MADNESS!

SEEMS WE'RE ALMOST THERE. NOT A MINUTE TOO SOON!

I'D STILL BE CAREFUL IF I WERE YOU.

THEY KNOW IT'S THE END OF THE TRIP TOO.

THEY CAN FEEL THE WINDS O' FREEDOM OR ESCAPE. THEY'V' NEVER BEEN SO JUMPY.

THURSDAY, 17 JANUARY 1788.
ARRIVAL IN BOTANY BAY.

OVER THERE, SIR!

HO!

I THINK THEY'RE JUST PLANNING TO WATCH US.

LET'S START BY EXPLORING THE SURROUNDINGS. BUT STAY ALERT.

WHAT DO YOU SAY, ARTHUR? WHAT ARE THEY REALLY THINKING?

HARD TO TELL. IT'S BEEN EIGHTEEN YEARS SINCE THEY'VE SEEN WHITE MEN ON THEIR TERRITORY.

IF THEY EVEN REMEMBER CAPTAIN COOK...

343

AS I FEARED.

THE SOIL'S DRY, ARID. YOU CAN TELL AT A GLANCE. HOW WILL WE EVER GROW THINGS HERE?

A BIT FURTHER ON, MAYBE?

NO, LIEUTENANT. WE CAN'T SET UP TOO FAR INTO THE THICKETS.

IMAGINE THE WORK IT'D TAKE TO FELL THESE TREES AND MAKE CAMP!

AND WE MUST STAY CLOSE TO THE WATER. WE NEED A PORT.

GOOD LORD, HOW COULD COOK HAVE BEEN SO BLIND?

MEE DiEE!

KEEP YOUR MEN AT THE READY. YOU NEVER KNOW...

WHALLOO.

RIFLES AT THE READY. GENTLY, LADS...

NGALU PIYALA... WAWI... WUNGARA.

LET 'EM HAVE A GOOD LOOK OR I'LL CLAP YO[U] IN IRONS! I MEAN IT!

WANGARA...

MULLABO.

WURULBADYAOU.

NHAING... WE-RE... GUAUAGO...

ALL RIGHT, GET DRESSED. I THINK THEY'VE SEEN ENOUGH.

POW!

DIDY! DIDY!!!!

I DIDN'T WANT IT TO COME TO THIS, BUT WHAT ELSE WAS THERE TO DO?

WELL, EACH THING IN ITS OWN TIME. OUR FIRST PRIORITY: FOUND A COLONY.

BACK ABOARD THE SUPPLY SHIP GENTLEMEN!

BUT I DO INDEED WONDER WHAT LIVING WITH THEM WILL BE LIKE.

"MY DEAR BETSY, FINALLY WE ALL ARRIVED AT BOTANY BAY..."

"THE SHIPS IN B DIVISION WERE ONLY TWO DAYS BEHIND US."

"HOW UNFOUNDED WERE THE GOVERNOR'S FEARS! HE REALLY ISN'T THE BEST SAILOR IN THE WORLD."

"AND AS IF THAT WEREN'T ENOUGH, WE LEARNED BOTANY BAY WASN'T TO BE OUR FINAL DESTINATION."

"THERE ISN'T ENOUGH FRESH WATER THERE, AND THE SOIL'S NO GOOD FOR FARMING."

"THE BAY DOESN'T SHELTER OUR SHIPS FROM THE SWELL BROUGHT ON BY STRONG WESTERLY WINDS."

"MEANWHILE, MAKESHIFT STRUCTURES HAVE BEEN SET UP NONETHELESS."

"WE'LL HAVE TO GET USED TO EATING FISH MUCH MORE OFTEN."

"THE NATIVES WATCH US FROM A DISTANCE."

"CONTACT WITH THEM IS FREQUENT, AND THIS MORNING, WE SHOWED THEM THE[RE] WERE COLOURED MEN AMONG US AS WELL[.]"

"WHICH SEEMED TO REALLY SURPRISE THEM!"

NGANA!

"IT SEEMS THAT STRANGE AND FANTASTICAL ANIMALS HAVE BEEN SPOTTED IN THE WOODS."

"BUT THE HEAT AND UNCERTAINTY WEIGH UPON US."

"HAVE WE CO[ME] ALL THIS WAY [FOR] NOTHING?"

I DON'T KNOW ABOUT YOU, BUT ALL THESE BAYS SEEM BETTER SUITED TO OUR NEEDS.

INDEED.

PLUS THEY OFFER SEVERAL POSSIBLE SPOTS FOR SAFE ANCHOR.

LET'S LOOK AT THAT ONE. IT SEEMS FAIRLY LARGE AND EVEN BETTER PROTECTED THAN THE OTHERS.

GENTLEMEN, I THINK WE SHOULD CONGRATULATE OURSELVES ON HAVING FOUND THE FINEST NATURAL HARBOUR IN THE WORLD.

SAFETY FOR THE BOATS, FRESH WATER, GREENERY, SHELTER FROM THE SEA: HOW COULD WE FARE BETTER?

LISTEN UP!

WE'VE REACHED OUR FINAL DESTINATION! THIS IS IT!

I HEREBY NAME THIS BAY SYDNEY, THE MAN UNDER WHOSE AUTHORITY WE SET SAIL.

WHAT'S THIS NONSENSE?

SEE FOR YOURSELF! TWO SHIPS RIGHT OUTSIDE BOTANY BAY!

FLYING FRENCH FLAGS!

CALLED THE BOUSSOLE AND THE ASTROLABE, SIR.

OH, GOOD GOD! IT'S LA PÉROUSE'S EXPEDITION!

"I'VE EXAMINED IT FROM EVERY ANGLE. THERE'S NO OTHER WAY."

"LA PÉROUSE IS NO DOUBT AN EXCEPTIONAL NAVIGATOR, AN EXPLORER WORTHY OF COOK, A PIONEER IN EXPANDING OUR KNOWLEDGE OF THE WORLD..."

"BUT I MUST TREAT HIM AS AN ENEMY."

"THE STAKES ARE TOO HIGH."

"HE'S BLOCKING MY WAY OUT OF BOTANY BAY, BUT TOMORROW I'LL GET BY NO MATTER THE COST!"

"NOR WILL I MEET WITH HIM. I MUST SHOW HIM MY DETERMINATION, PROPRIETY BE DAMNED!"

MONSIEUR LA PÉROUSE? IS THAT YOU?

MR. SMITH! WHAT A NICE SURPRISE!

WHAT A SMALL WORLD! HOW WELL I RECALL OUR LITTLE CHAT IN THAT TAVERN IN PARIS.

MY TEETH ARE ALMOST GONE, AND MY HAIR TOO, I'M AFRAID.

WHAT DO OWE THE ONOUR, PTAIN?

JOHN HUNTER, SIR.

CAPTAIN OF THE SIRIUS, COMMANDER OF THE FLEET...

AND GOVERNOR, SHOULD ANYTHING BEFALL MR. PHILLIP, THE HONOUR'S MINE.

GOVERNOR PHILLIP LEFT THIS MORNING, IF I'M NOT MISTAKEN.

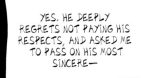

YES. HE DEEPLY REGRETS NOT PAYING HIS RESPECTS, AND ASKED ME TO PASS ON HIS MOST SINCERE—

I UNDERSTAND THE SITUATION. YOU'RE LAYING CLAIM TO A TERRITORY AND YOU'RE AFRAID I'LL INTERFERE.

I'M DISTURBING YOUR PLANS!

LET'S SAY IT'S NOT THE BEST TIMING.

I HAVE NO PRETENSIONS TO POLITICS OR TERRITORIAL SOVEREIGNTY.

THIS IS A SCIENTIFIC EXPEDITION AIMED AT EXPLORING NEW LANDS AND MAKING BETTER MAPS.

THAT'S MY MISSION FROM THE KING OF FRANCE.

IF I MAY, SIR, HOW IS YOUR VOYAGE GOING?

BADLY.

I LOST 21 MEN ALMOST TWO YEARS AGO AT PORT DES FRANÇAIS, AND ANOTHER 12 IN SAMOA, FOUR MONTHS AGO.

INCLUDING MY DEAR FRIEND DE LANGLE, CAPTAIN OF THE ASTROLABE.

I'M SORRY...

MERCI.

REST ASSURED, WE'LL DO EVERYTHING WE CAN TO MAKE YOUR STAY HERE EASIER.

ARE YOU SO AFRAID I WON'T LEAVE, MR. HUNTER?

ALL I ASK IS THE RIGHT TO DROP ANCHOR FOR A FEW WEEKS IN BOTANY BAY, AND GATHER A FEW SUPPLIES.

THEN I'LL HEAD BACK TO THE PACIFIC.

DROPPING ANCHOR IS FINE, AS ARE WOOD AND FRESH WATER.

ALAS, WE HAVE BUT LITTLE FOOD OURSELVES. OUR SITUATION IS JUST AS DIRE, BELIEVE ME.

H.

OF COURSE. I UNDERSTAND.

WHERE ARE YOU HEADED NEXT?

NEW CALEDONIA, NEW GUINEA, NEW HOLLAND, THE GULF OF CARPENTERIA, THEN DOUBLING BACK TO VAN DIEMEN'S LAND.

AND THEN FRANCE! I HOPE TO ARRIVE BY DECEMBER 1788.

WHAT DO YOU THINK LIES BETWEEN NEW SOUTH WALES AND NEW HOLLAND?

THAT'S THE QUESTION!

YOU'LL HAVE SPENT THREE YEARS AT SEA!

AND OF THOSE THREE YEARS, THERE WAS BUT ONE DAY WHEN I MIGHT HAVE SPOKEN WITH CAPTAIN PHILLIP.

BUT I'LL NEVER HAVE THE PRIVILEGE, I SUPPOSE.

MR. HUNTER, THANK THE GOVERNOR FOR ME, AND ASSURE HIM I'LL BE GONE IN A FEW WEEKS.

Book III
Bandaiyan

"Hear me, white men! An ancient forebear was my race
Of olden men who, far from the sun's new face,
Our gods did bear on wings of gale and squall
to the lonely isle that lightning holds in thrall."

Charles-Marie Leconte de Lisle
(Final Posthumous Poems, 1895)

THE BUSH. A STRANGE NAME FOR....

THE VAST...

YONDER.

ONE SYLLABLE BRISTLING WITH INFINITE MEANING.

HE'D RUN A LONG WAY.

FLED.

OR SO HE THOUGHT.

HOW LONG NOW?

TWO DAYS?

WHEN WOULD....

HE BE CAUGHT? HIS BROAD BLACK BACK'S A TARGET FOR THE WHITES.

HE BRAVED THE BUSH AND ALL ITS MANY PESTS.

AMIDST THE FLIES HE TRIES TO STEAL SOME SLEEP.

THAT NO ONE'S COME A-HUNTING YET SUGGESTS....

HIS ENEMIES ARE THOSE THAT CRAWL AND CREEP.

O BRAVE NEW WORLD, THAT HAS SUCH MONSTERS IN'T!

MAKE ME ANGRY AND I'LL GET REALLY MEAN.

NGAMA WE-RE....

LEAVE ME BE, YOU SAVAGES!

CLEAR OFF!

PARRIBUGO KA-MI BERANG....

THAT'S RIGHT....

HUH? NO, NO, NO, NO! NO WAY!

WASN'T A REQUEST, JOHN.

HEAR ME, CRYBABY?

YANK OUT THIS SPIKE NOW AND PROVE YOU'RE A MAN!

I HELPED YOU, PROTECTED YOU.

WITHOUT ME, YOU'D BE SOME PERVERT'S PRETTY BOY.

I'VE NEVER ASKED YOU FOR ANYTHING BEFORE.

I... I DON'T KNOW—

DO IT!

AAAAHHH !

STOP.

WHAT? WHAT'S WRONG?

HIDE, QUICK! GET IN THERE!

WHAT THE—?

SHUT YOUR TRAP!

389

WHAT'S
THAT SAVAGE
UP TOP?

SHH!

"WHAT THE HELL WAS THAT? HE JUST KILLED HIS KID RIGHT BEFORE OUR EYES."

DAMMIT, CAESAR, SAY SOMETHING!

D'YE THINK I'M BLIND!

I DON'T KNOW THEIR CUSTOMS!

DON'T YOU THINK THEY'D BE SHOCKED IF WE HANGED A MAN IN FRONT OF THEM?

TALK ABOUT BARBARITY...

I DON'T KNOW IF I CAN MAKE IT IN THIS HELL. I REALLY DON'T.

JUNE 1789.

WE CAN'T GO ON LIKE THIS!

THEFTS ARE MULTIPLYING. OUR MEN ARE WOUNDED.

THE SLIGHTEST FORAY AFIELD AND MY MEN RISK DEATH OR IMPALEMENT ON A DAMNED SPEAR!

AND YET IT IS YOU, MAJOR, WHO REPRESENT STRENGTH, LAW, AND ORDER!

AND YOU HAVE CLOTHES, RIFLES, AND POWDER!

ALL THEY HAVE ARE BARE BODIES...

AND SPEARS, AS YOU SAY, WHICH ARE BUT POINTED STICKS. THEIR FEAR OF US—

DON'T GO FAVOURING THE WRONG SIDE NOW, I BEG YOU.

401

WELL, WELL, LOOK WHO IT IS.

BLACK CAESAR AND JOHN HUDSON.

YES, SIR! WE CAUGHT THEM AT LAST.

THESE IDIOTS MADE IT EASY FOR US. THEY WERE GOING ROUND IN CIRCLES UP ON ROSE HILL.

YOU TWO DISAPPOINT ME DEEPLY. WHAT DID YOU HOPE TO FIND IN FLEEING?

CAT GOT YOUR TONGUE, HUDSON?

NO, THAT'S NOT IT, SIR.

ACTUALLY, I FOLLOWED CAESAR. ON A WHIM, DIDN'T THINK. PLEASE BELIEVE ME, SIR!

AM I BOTHERING YOU, REVEREND JOHNSON?

NOT AT ALL, GOVERNOR, PLEASE.

COME IN!

I REALLY APPRECIATED YOUR SERMON LAST SUNDAY.

THE COLONY LISTENED ATTENTIVELY.

DID YOU NOTICE IT WAS BASED ON PSALM 116, VERSE 12?

"WHAT SHALL I RENDER UNTO THE LORD FOR ALL HIS BENEFITS TOWARD ME?"

EXACTLY! A QUESTION THAT APPLIES DIRECTLY TO ALL OF US HERE.

BUT SO FEW KNOW IT.

I USED THAT VERSE AS AN EPIGRAPH TO MY FIRST SERVICE ON SUNDAY, 3 FEBRUARY 1788. I REMEMBER IT AS IF IT WERE YESTERDAY.

SO MANY THINGS HAVE HAPPENED SINCE WE LANDED...

OUR PERCEPTION OF TIME DIFFERS FUNDAMENTALLY DEPENDING ON THE HEMISPHERE, DON'T YOU THINK?

YOU ASK ME, IT'S BEING SEDENTARY OR NOMADIC THAT CHANGES OUR RELATIONSHIP TO TIME MORE THAN GEOGRAPHICAL POSITION.

AND OUR PERCEPTION OF GOD?

THAT FLUCTUATES TOO, I SUPPOSE.

I'M ALWAYS ASTONISHED TO SEE HOW WELL SUPPLIED YOU ARE FOR SETTLING THIS NEW COLONY.

HOW MANY BOOKS DID YOU BRING?

100 BIBLES, 100 PRAYER BOOKS, 400 NEW TESTAMENTS, AND 500 PSALTERS, AMONG OTHERS.

I'D LIKE TO OPEN A LIBRARY SOON, WHERE I MIGHT LEND THEM. WHAT DO YOU THINK?

A LAUDABLE GESTURE.

BUT YOU MIGHT HAVE A HARD TIME CIRCULATING YOUR 50 COPIES OF THE DANGERS OF PERJURY.

OR YOUR 100 COPIES OF EXHORTATIONS TO CHASTITY.

IS THAT A REBUKE? SOMETIMES I FEEL YOU STRAY FAR FROM THE LORD'S PATH.

I TRY NOT TO, FOR I FIND IT TO BE A FACTOR [OF] SOCIAL COHESION.

LET'S JUST SAY I'M... PRAGMATIC.

BESIDES, I'D LIKE TO DISCUSS A DECISIO[N] I'M ABOUT TO MAKE.

I'M LISTENING.

410

416

HEY, COME AND LOOK! THEY CAUGHT SOME INDIANS!

EH? YOU SURE?

AYE, RIGHT SURE, YOU CAN SEE THEM IN THE BOAT COMING BACK!

I ALREADY TOLD YOU, THEY AREN'T INDIANS! INDIANS ARE FROM INDIA. I DON'T EVEN KNOW WHERE WE ARE, REALLY.

THE TYKE'S RIGHT. LOOKS LIKE THE COLONY JUST GOT TWO NEW PRISONERS.

MOVE ALONG! NOTHING TO SEE HERE! BACK TO WORK!

JUST A QUICK LOOK, SERGEANT! DOESN'T HAPPEN EVERY DAY!

ALL RIGHT, TILL THEY GET OFF. THEN... I'M WARNING YOU!

FIRST TIME I'VE SEEN 'EM SO CLOSE!

THE FURTHER OFF, THE BETTER, SAYS I!

STROLLING AROUND ALL NAKED LIKE THAT...

AND THAT SMELL!

WE'RE BACK AND REPORTING FOR DUTY, SIR!

ATTENTION!

MEE DIEE!

UR REPORT, LIEUTENANT!

SIR! YES, SIR!

THIS MORNING WE HEADED OUT TO MANLY BEACH. WE STAYED HIDDEN MOST OF THE DAY AND THESE TWO SHOWED UP ALL ALONE IN A CANOE.

WE CAPTURED THEM FAIRLY EASILY. CHANCE ALONE DECIDED THEIR FATE. NO ONE WAS WOUNDED.

YOU DID WELL NOT TO SEPARATE THEM. WE WILL KEEP THEM BOTH WITH THE COLONY, AND ENCOURAGE THEM TO FIT IN.

YES, SIR! MISSION ACCOMPLISHED, SIR!

I KNOW HOW HARD THIS WAS FOR YOU, LIEUTENANT.

SOLDIERS! ATTEN-TION! RIGHT TURN!

YOU MAY STEP OUT NOW, GENTLEMEN.

A PERFECT DEMONSTRATION OF AUTHORITY!

IT WAS NECESSARY THAT THEY SEE YOU, SIR, AS THE CHIEF REPRESENTATIVE OF THIS COLONY.

THE LEADER.

MOREOVER...

THEY ALREADY CALL YOU "BE-ANNA". I KNOW THIS WORD.

IT MEANS "FATHER".

INTERESTING! I MYSELF AM READY TO CONSIDER THEM FULLY-FLEDGED MEMBERS OF OUR CAMP...

IRRESPECTIVE OF THEIR COLOUR AND RACE!

SINCE THEY CALL ME "FATHER", I SHALL THEM BOTH "SON".

THEY'RE YOURS.

YOU ARE TASKED WITH TEACHING THEM ENGLISH.

ONLY YOU TWO ARE FIT FOR THE JOB.

THE FASTER THE BETTER, NATURALLY.

FORGIVE ME, BUT... DURING THE DAY...

ARE THEY FREE TO GO WHERE THEY WANT AND DO AS THEY PLEASE?

OF COURSE NOT.

A CONVICT HAS BEEN DESIGNATED TO ACCOMPANY THEM AT ALL TIMES.

BESIDES, THEY'LL BE CHAINED TOGETHER BY IRONS.

LIEUTENANT CLARK?

YES?

MARY BROAD, IS IT?

IT'S BRYANT NOW. I MARRIED LAST YEAR.

OH, YES! I REMEMBER.

YOURS WAS ONE OF THE FIRST WEDDINGS CELEBRATED IN THIS NEW LAND.

HOW'S YOUR DAUGHTER?

CHARLOTTE? SHE'S HEALTHY, GROWING WELL.

WE LIVE IN A LITTLE TENT A BIT HIGHER UP.

YES, I HEARD YOUR HUSBAND WAS PUT IN CHARGE OF FISHING.

GOOD. ONE MUST GAIN A NEW PURCHASE ON LIFE.

I DON'T KNOW... I MISS MY HOME.

NO, I SUPPOSE NOT.

IT'S NOT LIKE WE'RE ALLOWED TO FORGET WE'RE CRIMINALS!

WHAT'S THAT SOLDIER DOING HERE?

HE COME TO EYE THE LADIES FOR A WEE SNACK?

HE PROBABLY THINKS HE CAN HELP HIMSELF TO A CLAM OR TWO!

RATHER DIE THAN TWO-BACK IT WITH A REDBACK, SAYS I.

WHAT'S GOT INTO YOU? I NEVER ASKED YOU FOR ANYTHING!

YOU'D BETTER WATCH YOUR TONGUE OR YOU'LL END UP IN IRONS!

HE'S ALL MOUTH AND NO TROUSERS!

JAILS, WHIPS, IRONS, BULLYING, AND PUNISHMENT — THAT'S ALL THEY KNOW!

WE KNOW YOUR KIND, LARK! YOU'VE GOT NO BALLS! YOUR WIFE BACK HOME SAY SHE'D WAIT FOR YOU?

IF I WAS HERE, I'D BE LOOKING AROUND TOO. YOU KNOW, SO I DON'T LOSE MY TOUCH. HA HA!

CUCKOLD!

YOU LOT... YOU'RE ALL...

I'M ASHAMED OF YOU!

WE SURELY DID PROVOKE HIM.

IT WON'T HURT HIM. HE'S HARDLY THE WORST OF 'EM, BUT HE DOES NEED OBEDIENT LITTLE SHREW TO KEEP HIM SWE

HE WOULDN'T BE SO UPTIGHT!

YOU MUSTN'T LISTEN TO EVERYTHING THEY SAY, YOU KNOW.

THEY JUST WANTED TO TEASE YOU.

I COULD LOCK 'EM ALL UP ON DRY BREAD IF I WANTED!

BUT YOU WON'T.

NO... THERE ARE MORE IMPORTANT MATTERS IN THIS COLONY, I THINK.

EACH IN ITS TIME.

YOU ARE...?

MY NAME'S MARY. MARY BRANHAM.

AND I KNOW YOUR NAME IS RALPH, LIEUTENANT CLARK!

MAY I SIT AND TALK WITH YOU A WHILE?

I NEED SOME AIR. THE WALK FROM THE ROCKS IS FAIRLY TIRING IN THIS HEAT.

SIT DOWN, RALPH.

ONCE MORE, CHRISTMAS WAS CELEBRATED UNDER THE HEAT, SUN, AND MOSQUITOES. THE WEEKS WENT BY, BUT THERE WAS NEVER LESS WORK.

THERE WERE ALWAYS TREES TO BE CUT, HOUSES TO BE BUILT, LAND TO BE READIED, SECTORS MEASURED OFF, CROPS ATTEMPTED...

THE COLONY WAS ON ITS OWN. EVERY WEEK, FOOD AND DRINK RATIONS GOT SMALLER.

BUT ALREADY IT LOOKED NOTHING LIKE THE WILD, UNTAMED AREAS FROM TWO YEARS AGO.

WITH TINY, BABY STEPS, A RADICAL TRANSFORMATION OF THE LANDSCAPE WAS UNDERWAY.

COLBEE HAD ESCAPED FROM THE CAMP IN JANUARY 1790. HIS "GUARD" HAD BEEN SEVERELY PUNISHED.

BENNELONG REMAINED ON HIS OWN, A FAMILIAR SIGHT, WALKING AROUND IN IRONS, A SAD LOOK ON HIS FACE.

GOVERNOR PHILLIP WAS SOMETHING OF A RECLUSE IN HIS HOUSE, WITH HIS HOUSEKEEPER MRS. BROOKS.

THEY WERE SUSPECTED OF HAVING AN AFFAIR.

NO ONE KNEW WHAT LAY BEYOND THE BUSH. NO DOUBT TERRA INCOGNITA WITH "AB ORIGINES", BUT ALSO OTHER PEOPLES AND STILL MORE WILD ANIMALS, OR MAYBE EVEN BLUE MOUNTAINS. WHO KNEW?

FINALLY, BENNELONG WAS ALLOWED TO MOVE ABOUT WITHOUT IRONS IN APRIL 1790, FIVE MONTHS AFTER HIS CAPTURE. HE WAS "PART OF THE FURNITURE", AS IT WERE. TRULY, ALL HOPE OF A BETTER UNDERSTANDING BETWEEN PEOPLES RESTED ON HIS SHOULDERS.

REPEAT AFTER ME.

GOODBYE! EASY, RIGHT?

"GOODBYE". WHAT'S THAT MEAN?

WE SAY GOODBYE WHEN WE LEAVE SOMEONE, BUT KNOW WE'LL SEE HIM AGAIN. WITH A LITTLE WAVE.

GOODBYE! IS FUN!

DO YOU HAVE THE SAME THING?

YURABOAALO, ALMOST SAME THING!

YURA— WHAT?

YURA-BOA-ALO.

YURA-BOA-ALO.

GOOD.

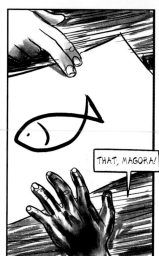

DO YOU LIKE IT HERE?

F ME LIKE HERE WITH YOU? YES, BUT... HOW YOU SAY... I TJERABARRBO-WARYAOU!

HUH? WHAT'S THAT MEAN?

TJERA-BARRBO-WARY-AOU... I MUST NOT BECOME WHITE. I AM MAN OF HERE. I EORA!

EORA, YES...

I THINK GOODBYE AGAIN. CAN ALSO SAY WEEANADOOROO!

SLOWER, PLEASE? WEENA— OHH, I CAN'T DO IT!

IT'S TOTALLY DIFFERENT FROM YURABOLO!

YURABOAALO!

RIGHT, THAT'S IT. I'M ALL MIXED UP. WHAT'S THE DIFFERENCE?

443

444

FOR THE GOVERNOR, IT'S ONLY POLITICAL.

I FEEL LIKE WE'RE THE ONLY TWO WHO REALLY WANT TO KNOW THESE PEOPLE AND THEIR LANGUAGE BETTER.

GOVERNOR... BE-ANNA! HOW IS HE?

SHOULDN'T SAY THIS, BUT I THE FEELING HE DREAMS OF GOING BACK TO ENGLAND. NO DOUBT HE DEEMS HIS MISSION ACCOMPLISHED AFTER BRINGING US HERE.

EXCEPT THAT RIGHT NOW IS THE HARDEST PART!

EVERYTHING NEEDS BUILDING, SHORING UP! AND HE ALONE GUARANTEES OUR UNITY!

I AGREE COMPLETELY. BUT HE WAS A SAILOR BEFORE BECOMING A GOVERNOR. IF THE VOYAGE WAS A CHALLENGE FOR HIM, ADMINISTRATION IS A BURDEN.

S, I UNDERSTAND. 'S A MAN OF ACTION, OT MANAGEMENT.

NOT TO MENTION THE FAMINE AND ANARCHY CONSTANTLY THREATENING OUR FRAGILE COLONY.

WE MUST HOPE THE CROPS SOON BEAR FRUIT.

AS FOR ANARCHY, AS YOU SAY, THE GOVERNOR HAS A FEW IDEAS FOR LAYING DOWN THE LAW.

THAT'S WHY I CAME TO SEE YOU, ACTUALLY, MR. SMITH, MR. BENNELONG, IF YOU'LL FOLLOW ME, PLEASE.

447

AND THUS, FOR THE CRIME OF FRUIT AND VEGETABLE THEFT AGAINST A COLONY STILL FIGHTING FAMINE...

WHERE ALL FOODSTUFFS MUST BE STOCKED, RATIONED, AND SHARED, DO WE NOW SOLEMNLY COMMEND YOUR SOUL TO GOD.

EXECUTIONER, DO YOUR DUTY!

MERCY! I WAS TOO HUNGRY! I WON'T DO IT AGAIN!

WHY ROPE AROUND HIS NECK?

ALAS, MY FRIEND, YOU'LL FIND OUT SOON ENOUGH. BRACE YOURSELF.

IN THEE, O LORD, DO I PUT MY TRUST: LET ME NEVER BE PUT TO CONFUSION. DELIVER ME IN THY RIGHTEOUSNESS, AND CAUSE ME TO ESCAPE: INCLINE THINE EAR UNTO ME, AND SAVE ME.

MERCY! I BEG YOU!

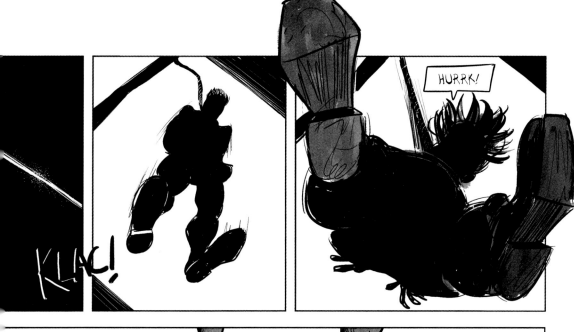

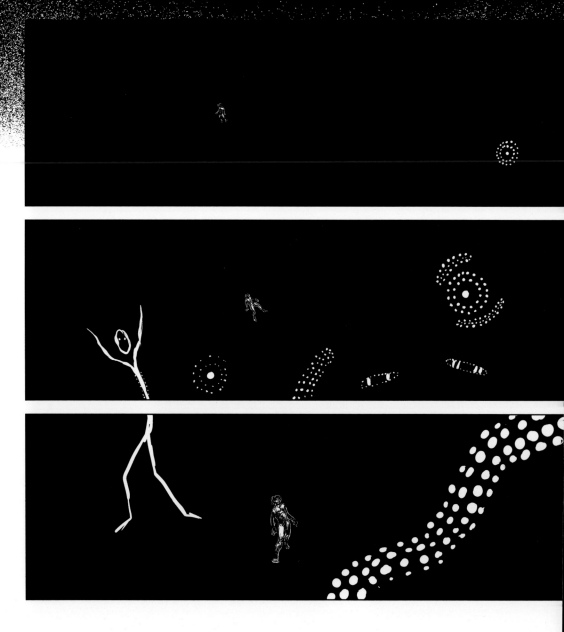

MAY 1790.

THANK YOU, SIR.

A TOAST IN YOUR HONOUR, MAJOR!

TO YOUR DEPARTURE AND YOUR NEW RESPONSIBILITIES!

THANK YOU, SIR. THOUGH YOU KNOW QUITE WELL I'D RATHER STAY IN PORT JACKSON.

COME, COME, YOU'RE NOT AGAINST THE IDEA OF RUNNING A NEW COLONY! IT SUITS YOU SO WELL!

FROM WHAT I KNOW, IT'S EVEN HARDER TO SETTLE ON NORFOLK ISLAND THAN IT IS HERE.

THE LAND'S NO GOOD, IT'S TOO WINDY, AND T SUBSOIL'S TOO DRY. FA FOR SURE!

NO ONE EVER CLAIMED STARTING A COLONY WAS EASY.

I'M NOT SURE OUR SITUATION HAS MUCH TO ENVY.

DID YOU KNOW A MAN DIED OF HUNGER LAST WEEK?

I DIDN'T WANT TO ANNOUNCE IT PUBLICLY. WE'RE NO BETTER OFF THAN YOU.

ALL I KNOW IS THE HIERARCHY OF AUTHORITY WILL BE RESPECTED.

I'LL COUNTENAN NO DISORDER C NORFOLK ISLAN

IS THAT A PERSONAL INSULT, MAJOR?

SIR! I WOULDN'T DREAM OF IT.

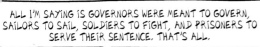

ALL I'M SAYING IS GOVERNORS WERE MEANT TO GOVERN, SAILORS TO SAIL, SOLDIERS TO FIGHT, AND PRISONERS TO SERVE THEIR SENTENCE. THAT'S ALL.

QUITE A COLD SUMMARY OF HUMAN RELATIONS.

..AS, YOU KNOW AS WELL AS I THAT THE WORLD IS RULED BY LAW AND ORDER.

AS A RESULT, FEELINGS MUST NOT GET IN THE WAY WHEN YOU'VE A DUTY AND MISSION TO APPLY THEM!

I DON'T THINK I GAVE YOU LEAVE TO STAND.

WATCH YOURSELF, MAJOR!

YOU LEAVE TOMORROW MORNING.

YES, SIR!

AND YOUR COMMAND SHALL REMAIN IN EFFECT UNTIL SUCH TIME AS A NEW OFFICER ARRIVES WITH MISSION ORDERS...

DULY SIGNED BY MYSELF OR AN AUTHORITY REPRESENTING NEW SOUTH WALES!

IS THAT QUITE CLEAR?

PERFECTLY, SIR. GOODBYE, SIR...

PERHAPS FOR EVER.

GOOD RIDDANCE!

THE GOVERNOR REMEMBERED BERNARD DE MALIEZ.

HE'D DIED A YEAR EARLIER, AT THE AGE OF 26.

THE ONLY FRENCHMAN IN THE COLONY.

ALMOST OUT OF BRAVADO, AND DESPITE ALL THE WARS BETWEEN THEIR NATIONS, HE'D MADE THE MAN HIS MAJORDOMO.

SOMETIMES THEY'D HAD DEEP, LIVELY DISCUSSIONS.

THE AMERICAS ARE INDEPENDENT, EXPLORERS ROAM THE OCEANS, NEW LANDS ARE BEING DISCOVERED — WE LIVE IN AN AGE OF REVOLUTION!

THIS FEELS FUNNY. NOT THAT WE'RE NOT USED TO IT, BUT STILL!

NOT TALKING, CAESAR?

DON'T WANT TO.

I ALWAYS WONDERED... DO YOU CONSIDER ME YOUR FRIEND?

NO.

AT LEAST YOU'RE HONEST, CAREFUL, CAESAR! YOU'LL WIND UP ALL ALONE, AND YOU WON'T LIKE IT.

I KNOW.

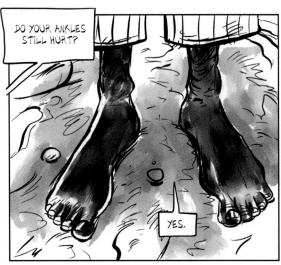

JUNE 1790.

HE'S BEEN MISSING FOR TWO DAYS. AS YOU CAN IMAGINE, I'VE LOOKED EVERYWHERE.

I KNEW IT. HE PULLED A COLBEE ON US.

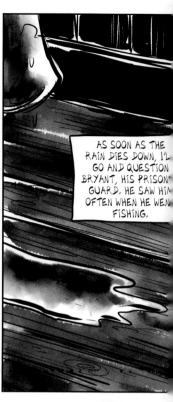

AS SOON AS THE RAIN DIES DOWN, I'L GO AND QUESTION BRYANT, HIS PRISON GUARD. HE SAW HIM OFTEN WHEN HE WEN FISHING.

I CAN'T BELIEVE HE'D JUST LEAVE US LIKE THAT!

HE'D MADE ENORMOUS PROGRESS RECENTLY.

WHO ARE WE TO AND UNDERSTA THEM?

475

Epilogue

LOOK! A BOAT!

ON 6 JUNE 1790, THE LADY JULIANA, FIRST SHIP F THE 2ND FLEET, REACHED PORT JACKSON.

ABOARD: MORE THAN 200 FEMALE CONVICTS.

"WOMEN INSTEAD OF SUPPLIES", REMARKED DAVID COLLINS.

"WHORES", DECLARED LIEUTENANT CLARK.

THE GROWING COLONY WAS STRUGGLING WITH FAMINE AND DESPAIR.

BUT LONDON, ON TO A GOOD THING AND UNDETERRED BY SCRUPLES, FREELY SCATTERED ITS BAD SEEDS TO THE FAR END OF THE WORLD.

QUITE NATURALLY, POVERTY AND PENURY WERE REBORN AND THRIVED ANEW.

EXCEPT THAT THIS TIME, THERE WAS NOWHERE LEFT TO GO.

IN JULY AND AUGUST 1790, A WHALE LOST ITS WAY IN THE PACIFIC, SPENDING SEVERAL DAYS ASTRAY IN THE VARIOUS COVES OF PORT JACKSON...

SOWING PANIC AMONG THE INEXPERIENCED FISHING CREWS...

BEFORE BEACHING ITSELF AT LAST ON A RATHER PRETTY BEACH NORTHWEST OF THE COLONY'S MAIN TERRITORY.

PHILLIP HAD ONCE VISITED THAT SHORE.

IMPRESSED BY THE SIZE AND STOUTNESS OF THE NATIVES THERE, HE HAD NAMED IT "MANLY".

THAT WAS WHERE HE CHANCED UPON BENNELONG, AMONG HIS OWN KIND.

HE HAD NOT CHANGED SINCE FLEEING THE CAMP.

HE EVEN LOOKED UPON THE GOVERNOR WITH KINDNESS, AS BEFORE.

BUT THINGS NEVER STAY THE SAME.

A NATIVE BY THE NAME OF WILLEMERIN SUDDENLY BRANDISHED HIS SPEAR...

AND AIMED AT THE ENGLISHMEN, WITH NO FEAR OF BEING FIRED UPON.

THE PAIN WAS SO SHARP HE DID NOT EVEN CRY OUT.

HE THOUGHT HIMSELF DEAD, BUT FELT THE SAND BENEATH HIS KNEES.

HE WAS CARRIED OFF IN A WILD PANIC. IT WAS THOUGHT HE WOULD NOT SURVIVE THE NIGHT.

IN FACT, HIS CONVALESCENCE LASTED SEVERAL WEEKS.

COLLINS SHOULDERED THE IMPOSING BURDEN OF MANAGING THE COLONY'S AFFAIRS.

PRIVATELY, HE WOULD SAY HE WAS ALREADY DOING AS MUCH BEFORE THE GOVERNOR'S INJURY.

WHICH WAS TRUE.

REMORSE? GUILT? COMPASSION?

BENNELONG CAME BACK TO SEE PHILLIP AND ASK AFTER HIS HEALTH.

DEEP DOWN, THEY LIKED EACH OTHER WITHOUT REALLY KNOWING EACH OTHER, KNEW EACH OTHER WITHOUT SPEAKING MUCH, SPOKE TO EACH OTHER WITHOUT MUCH UNDERSTANDING.

CERTAIN TRUST HAD RETURNED TO THEM.

FOR HIS GUEST, PHILLIP HAD A LITTLE HOUSE BUILT BY THE WATER'S EDGE.

SEVERAL DECADES LATER, A GREAT WHITE OPERA HOUSE WAS ERECTED IN THAT VERY SPOT — JUST AS BENNELONG HAD DREAMED AND FEARED.

THE HOUSE WAS BOTH A DWELLING AND A REFUGE. THE NATIVE BROUGHT HIS FAMILY OVER.

A BIT FORCED AS INTEGRATIONS GO — BITTER, SHAKY.

NO ONE REALLY GOT WHAT THEY WANTED.

A DELICATE BALANCE BETWEEN THE FORCES RULING THE LAND.

ON *11 DECEMBER 1792*, PHILLIP LEFT SYDNEY, TO HIS RELIEF. HE FELT HIS TASK FINISHED. HIS HEALTH ALSO WORRIED HIM.

ABOVE ALL, HE WISHED TO REMIND THE ADMIRALTY OF HIS ACCOMPLISHMENTS. STAYING AWAY FROM LOND TOO LONG IS NEVER A GOOD WAY TO REAP HONOURS.

BENNELONG ACCOMPANIED HIM, DRESSED IN THE ENGLISH STYLE, WHICH MADE THE CREW LAUGH.

THE RETURN VOYAGE TOOK SIX MONTHS. EVERY DAY, BENNELONG MADE PROGRESS IN ENGLISH.

PHILLIP, HOWEVER, FAILED TO LEARN A SINGLE WORD OF THE EORA PEOPLE.

HE CLAIMED HE WAS TOO OLD TO START.

IN TRUTH, HE SIMPLY DID NOT WANT TO.

A FEW YEARS EARLIER, KING GEORGE III HAD TAKEN ILL.

HE WAS SUBJECT TO FITS OF MADNESS AND LOGORRHOEA.

HIS REIGN WAS TO LAST FOR ANOTHER 27 YEARS.

THE STATE OF THE COLONIES GREATLY PREOCCUPIED HIM.

HE HAD TAKEN THE AMERICANS' REBELLION AND INDEPENDENCE VERY BADLY.

HISTORY WOULD NOT REPEAT ITSELF WITH NEW SOUTH WALES.

AN EMPIRE HAD TO BE RULED WITH AN IRON FIST, REGARDLESS OF THE FRAGMENTS IT SOMETIMES LEFT BEHIND.

"THAT ENGLAND, THAT WAS WONT TO CONQUER OTHERS, HATH MADE A SHAMEFUL CONQUEST OF ITSELF," WROTE SHAKESPEARE.

A NATION TO MAKE ONE'S BLOOD RUN COLD, BOTH LITERALLY AND METAPHORICALLY.

FIFTEEN MONTHS AFTER REACHING LONDON, BENNELONG DECIDED TO RETURN TO HIS HOMELAND.

THE HOME OFFICE NEGOTIATED A PLACE FOR HIM ABOARD THE *RELIANCE*, HEADED FOR PORT JACKSON.

BUT HE HAD TO WAIT ANOTHER EIGHT MONTHS.

AT 56, EX-GOVERNOR PHILLIP WAS PREPARING TO REMARRY: A CERTAIN ISABELLA WHITEHEAD, AGED 45.

A MARRIAGE OF CONVENIENCE, OF COURSE.

AT LONG LAST, THE *RELIANCE* SET OUT TO BRAVE THE SEAS IN EARLY 1795.

AS THE NEW MRS. PHILLIP'S FATHER HAD SUDDENLY DIED, THE COUPLE FOUND THEMSELVES BLESSED WITH A COMFORTABLE FORTUNE.

THEY DECIDED TO SETTL DOWN IN THE CITY OF BAT

ALONE, AT A LOOSE END, ANXIOUS TO SEE HIS HOME AGAIN, BENNELONG WAS CONTINUALLY FASCINATED BY HIS HOSTS AND THEIR CUSTOMS.

THEY DRANK RUM, OFTEN AND AMPLY.

HE DRANK RUM, OFTEN AND AMPLY.

THE PHILLIPS ENTERTAINED EVERY WEEK IN THEIR SALON, FREQUENTED BY THE CREAM OF BATH SOCIETY.

THEY LISTENED TO THE GOVERNOR'S TALES OF STRANGE ANIMALS AND BLACK-SKINNED SAVAGES WITHOUT ALWAYS SEEING THE DIFFERENCE.

SEPTEMBER 1795. BENNELONG RETURNED TO PORT JACKSON, MORE COMMONLY KNOWN AS SYDNEY COVE. SOON IT WOULD SIMPLY BE SYDNEY.

OCTOBER 1795. ARTHUR PHILLIP IS BORED.

NOVEMBER 1795. HE KNOWS EVERYONE, BUT IS NO ONE'S FRIEND.

1796. HE RE-ENTERS THE SERVICE, DUE TO A NEW WAR WITH FRANCE. HE COMMANDS THE *ALEXANDER*, THE *SWIFTSURE*, THE *BLENHEIM*.

HE IS GIVEN ONLY RECONNAISSANCE MISSIONS WHILE OTHER ADMIRALS ARE CROWNED WITH LAURELS FOR ENGAGING NAPOLEON'S NAVY IN BATTLE.

1802. HE IS ALONE IN HIS HOUSE — PART OF THE FURNITURE, AS THEY SAY.

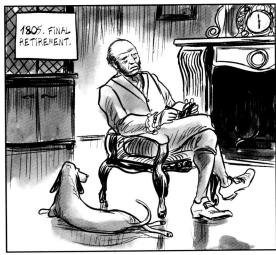

1805. FINAL RETIREMENT.

1807. FINAL REJECTION.

1808. A STROKE LEAVES HIM PARTIALLY PARALYSED.

1811. REELING DRUNK, RUM.

1812. "HIS" COLONY IS OFTEN IN HIS THOUGHTS.

1813. DEAD, FALLEN TO THE GROUND.

1814. DEAD, FALLEN FROM HIS WINDOW.

490

WILD.

FIERCE.

BURNING.

HOSTILE.

DISTANT.

ANCIENT.

THIS IS MY LAND, THE ONE I LOVE, THE ONE THAT HAUNTS ME.

I DO NOT ALWAYS RECOGNIZE IT.

TOO MUCH NOISE, TOO MANY CRIES, TOO MANY CASUALTIES.

THIS LIFE — I FLEE IT...

AND PLUNGE INTO MY TRUER TERRITORY, WHERE THE WIND WHISPERS OF MEN AND THEIR FABLES.

THESE FACES AND NAMES, METEORS IN A DARK SKY, BRIEF YET SHINING STARS STANDING OUT FROM THE REST...

JEAN-FRANÇOIS DE GALAUP, COMTE DE LA PÉROUSE, ILL AND EXHAUSTED AFTER A SCIENTIFIC VOYAGE OF ALMOST THREE YEARS AROUND THE GLOBE...

WHO REACHED BOTANY BAY JUST A BIT TOO LATE...

BY JUST A FEW HOURS...

WHO LEFT AGAIN WITHOUT A WORD, SO AS NOT TO DISTURB THE WELL-SETTLED ENGLISH: HE RAN AGROUND A FEW WEEKS LATER NEAR AN INHOSPITABLE ISLAND, THIS TIME CATASTROPHICALLY.

THE REMAINS OF THIS WRECK WERE FOUND ONLY 200 YEARS LATER, AN UNLUCKY HERO OF A CAUSE LOST TO TIME.

WATKIN TENCH, CAPTAIN-LIEUTENANT OF THE FIRST FLEET, A PARADOXICAL SOLDIER, CULTURED AND CURIOUS.

AFTER THE ATTACK ON PHILLIP AND THE MURDER OF THE COLONY'S GAME WARDEN A FEW MONTHS LATER, THE GOVERNOR DECIDED ON A PUNITIVE EXPEDITION AGAINST THE NATIVES.

TENCH'S ORDERS WERE TO CAPTURE TWO MEN FOR A PUBLIC HANGING.

HE WAS ALSO TO BRING BACK HEADS — ANY HEADS — FOR PUBLIC DISPLAY.

SO, AFTER BRAVING THE BUSH, BEARING THE HEAT...

AND EVEN ONCE AVOIDING QUICKSAND...

TENCH CLAIMED TO HAVE SEEN NO ONE. PHILLIP PRETENDED TO BELIEVE HIM.

ONCE BACK IN EUROPE, TENCH WAS IMPRISONED BY THE FRENCH AND FOUND HIMSELF IN A PRISON IN BRITTANY WITH ADMIRAL BLIGH, A COUSIN OF THE BOUNTY'S ALL TOO NOTORIOUS CAPTAIN.

THIS WAS HIS FINAL LINK WITH THE PACIFIC.

ROBERT ROSS. HARD-HEARTED, THICK-SKINNED. VICIOUS, OBTUSE, CRUEL, AUTHORITARIAN.

IN SHORT, A FAITHFUL SERVANT OF THE CROWN.

EVEN HIS ARRIVAL ON NORFOLK ISLAND CAUSED A FURORE, FOR THE *SIRIUS* RAN AGROUND AND SANK.

EVERYONE ESCAPED UNHARME INCLUDING HIM.

ONCE ON THE ISLAND, HIS REIGN FULFILLED EVERYONE'S WORST FEARS.

HE TRIED AN EXPERIMENT IN COOPERATIVE FARMING. THERE WAS THAT, AT LEAST. PHILLIP SOON RELIEVED HIM OF HIS DUTIES.

NO SOONER BACK IN SYDNEY IN DECEMBER *1791*, HE FOUGHT A DUEL. PHILLIP GOT RID OF HIM, AT LAST, A FEW DAYS LATER BY SENDING HIM BACK TO ENGLAND.

HE ENDED HIS LIFE DOING WHAT HE KNEW BEST: MAKING WAR.

HE SEEMS TO HAVE DIED IN *1808*.

494

RALPH CLARK. LIEUTENANT, ROMANTIC, LOVER, TORMENTED SOUL, PURITAN.

HE DID NOT MANAGE TO STAY FAITHFUL TO HIS WIFE TILL THE END — HIS DEAREST BETSY ALICIA.

MARY BRANHAM BECAME HIS MISTRESS.

ACCOMPANIED ROSS TO NORFOLK ISLAND, HOPING FOR PROMOTION. HE PUT UP WITH IT ALL, EMBRACING SERVILITY.

STILL, WHEN A WOMAN WAS PUBLICLY WHIPPED, HE CONSENTED TO STOP THE PUNISHMENT SHOULD SHE FAINT.

FROM WEAKNESS OR IMPUDENCE, HE NAMED HIS ILLEGITIMATE DAUGHTER ALICIA.

HE ALSO FOLLOWED ROSS WHEN HE LEFT FOR ENGLAND ABOARD THE GORGON.

FOUR YEARS EARLIER, HE HAD LEFT A WOMAN AND CHILD BEHIND HIM. HISTORY NOW REPEATED ITSELF.

HIS CONCLUSION? TERRA AUSTRALIS WAS NOT MEANT FOR HIM, SINCE VIRTUE AND MORALITY FOUND NO REWARD THERE.

HE HAD WRITTEN A GREAT DEAL DURING THE VOYAGE TO BOTANY BAY.

HE'D DREAMED A GREAT DEAL TOO...

AND EVEN SEEN THE FUTURE.

HIS WIFE DIED A FEW DAYS AFTER BRINGING A STILLBORN CHILD INTO THE WORLD IN 1794.

WITH HIS NINE-YEAR-OLD SON, RALPH JUNIOR, HE SET SAIL ON THE *TARTAR*, A WARSHIP HEADED FOR THE CARIBBEAN.

THE YOUNG BOY SUCCUMBED TO A BOUT OF VIOLENT FEVER.

THIS WAS THE LAST STRAW FOR CLARK, WHEN THE WORLD OF DREAMS — A NO-MAN'S-LAND SOME MYSTERIOUS ABILITY HAD LET HIM GLIMPSE — TOOK ON A TERRIBLE REALITY.

HE DIED THE SAME DAY AS HIS SON, FROM A SHOT STRAIGHT TO THE HEAD.

AND WHAT OF THE LITTLE CHIMNEY SWEEP?

JOHN HUDSON. CONVICTED CHILD. TRANSPORTED JUVENILE.

HIS DIRTY HANDPRINT ON A WALL COULD HAVE BEEN HIS SIGNATURE FOR POSTERITY.

WITH HIS YOUTH AND ＿HUSIASM, HE COULD HAVE ＿ONEERED A TERRITORIAL ＿OLUTION AS OTHERS LED ＿POLITICAL ONES.

O JOHN, ONCE YOUR ＿ONLY HORIZONS WERE ROOFS, CHIMNEYS, AND GAOL CELLS.

NOW YOU HAD TREES, RIVERS, SUNLIT COVES... EVERYTHING YOU NEEDED AT HAND TO TAKE FLIGHT!

YOU, TOO, LEFT FOR NORFOLK ISLAND IN MARCH 1790...

NEVER TO BE HEARD OF AGAIN.

JOHN, HOW DID YOU LOSE YOUR WAY?

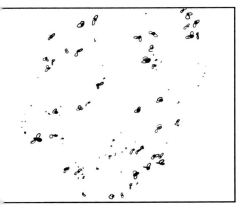

BLACK CAESAR, THE OUTLAW, THE BUSHRANGER.

EVER IN SEARCH OF A FREEDOM HE WOULD NEVER FIND.

"WE NEGROES, FORMER SLAVES, THE FORGOTTEN SOLDIERS OF REVOLUTIONS, THE GHOSTS OF WESTERN CAPITALS..."

"ONE DAY, I, CAESAR, WILL BE FREE AND IN THE DARK HOURS I WILL WALK IN GREAT WOODS THAT WILL WELCOME ME LIKE A NOMAD AND A MAN BLESSED."

"I WILL HAVE COME TO MY JOURNEY'S END, AND I WILL KNOW IT IS TIME TO LIVE AT LAST."

AND YET IN NORFOLK ISLAND HE MARRIED AND HAD TWO CHILDREN.

BACK IN SYDNEY IN 1793, THE FAMILY SETTLED DOWN PEACEABLY.

BUT TWO YEARS LATER, CAESAR WAS BACK AT IT. HE STOLE AND FLED. A PRICE WAS PUT ON HIS HEAD. THE HUNT LASTED THREE MONTHS.

HE WAS SHOT DOWN WITHOUT WARNING BY TWO BOUNTY HUNTERS.

AN END TO A LIFE OF WANDERING AND REVOLT.

HIS SOUL TOOK FLIGHT, PERHAPS AT PEACE.

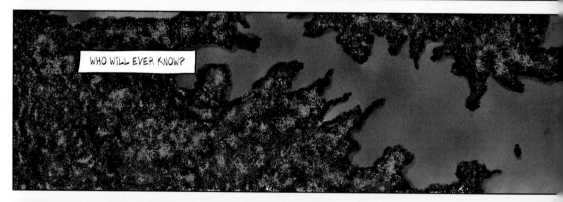

WHO WILL EVER KNOW?

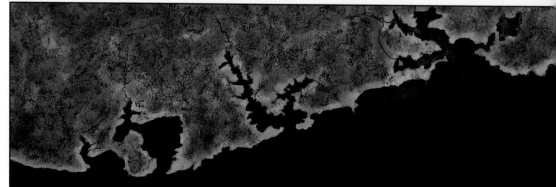

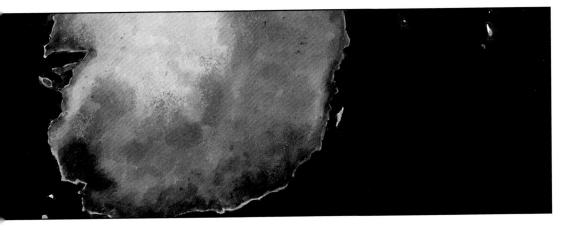

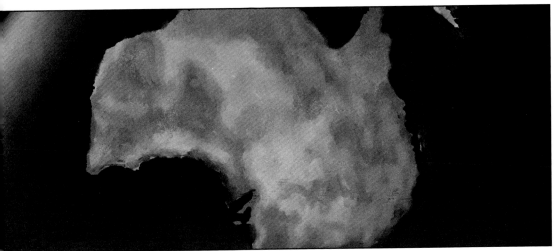

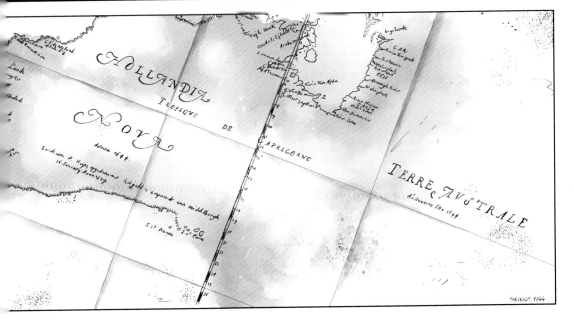

THEVENOT, 1644

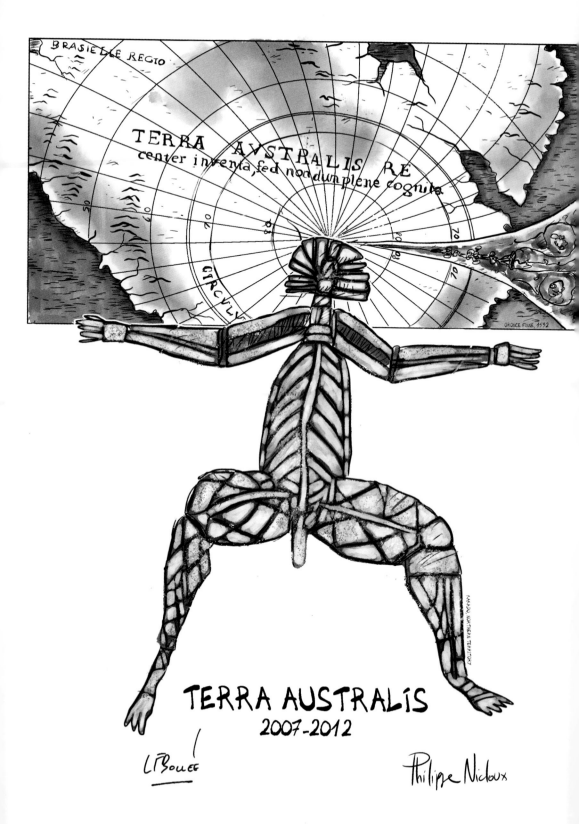

Bibliography

THE FIRST FLEET
Jonathan King
The Macmillan Company
of Australia Pty Ltd, 1982.

SYDNEY VIEWS 1788-1888
From the Beat Knoblauch Collection
Historic Houses Trust
of New South Wales, 2007.

AN ACCOUNT OF THE ENGLISH
COLONY IN NEW SOUTH WALES – Vol 1
David Collins
Project Gutenberg NSW – originally published by
T. Cadell Jun. & W. Davies,
London, 1798.

THE VOYAGE OF GOVERNOR PHILLIP
TO BOTANY BAY
Compilation
Project Gutenberg NSW – originally published by
John Stockdale, London, 1789.

A LONG WAY HOME
Mike Walker
Wiley, 2005.

DANCING WITH STRANGERS
Inga Clendinnen
Canongate, 2003.

A COMMONWEALTH OF THIEVES
Thomas Keneally
Anchor Books, 2007.

THE FATAL SHORE
Robert Hughes
Harvill, 1996.

ORPHANS OF HISTORY
Robert Holden
Text Publishing, 1999

BLACK FOUNDERS
Cassandra Pybus
UNSW Press, 2006.

THE FOUNDERS OF AUSTRALIA
A Biographical Dictionary of the First Fleet
Mollie Gillen

TOUR TO HELL
Convict Australia's Great Escape Myths
David Levell
University of Queensland Press, 2008.

BOUND FOR BOTANY BAY
Alan Brooke & David Brandon
The National Archives, 2005.

THE EXPLORERS
Tim Flannery
Grove Press, 1998.

ADMIRAL ARTHUR PHILLIP
The Man
Lyn M. Ferguson
Pilar Publishing, 2010.

BURIED ALIVE
Jack Egan
Allen & Unwin, 1999.

SYDNEY, FROM SETTLEMENT
TO THE BRIDGE
A Pictorial History
Ian Collis
New Holland Publishers, 2007.

THE FLOATING BROTHEL
Sian Rees
Review, 2001.

LA PÉROUSE,
LE GENTILHOMME DES MERS
Hans-Otto Meissner
Perrin, 1988.

LES DECOUVREURS
DU PACIFIQUE
Étienne Taillemite
Gallimard, 1987.

RELATIONS DE VOYAGES
AUTOUR DU MONDE
James Cook
La Découverte,
1988.

HISTOIRE DU PACIFIQUE
Dominique Barbe